HOW TO BECOME A

MILLION DOLLAR SPEAKER

THE STEVE SIEBOLD STORY

ELLIOT SALTZMAN

HOW TO BECOME A
MILLION DOLLAR SPEAKER

The STEVE SIEBOLD Story

by Elliot Saltzman

Published by London House

ISBN: 978-0-9755003-7-8

CREDITS

Cover and Book Design ~ Sandra Larson

DEDICATION

To my wife, Jennae, my biggest fan. You are the most amazing woman I know. Thanks for supporting me along the journey. I love you.

INTRODUCTION

When I was 23 years old, I quit everything I was doing and decided I was going to devote the next year to becoming a professional speaker. I had a message to share with the world and everyone around me encouraged me to go for it.

I built a website, put together a speech, and started selling myself as a speaker. I had 6 paid engagements lined up. I thought I was on fire and on my way to being the next big speaker. Then one night, I had a dream that I was speaking at my alma mater and I completely crashed and burned on stage in front of all my peers. The next morning I woke up and went to my computer to look for some kind of training. I googled professional speaker training and found a million different programs. So many were about becoming a better presenter and feeling more comfortable speaking in front of people. That's not what I needed. Others programs looked good, yet had no track record of producing any big name speakers. Then I discovered the Bill Gove Speech Workshop. It was a 62 year old workshop that was credited for training more million dollar speakers than any other program in history. The moment I saw the list of legends it had produced in the speaking business, I signed up.

When I attended the workshop, I was completely blown away. It literally took everything I thought I knew about speech writing and delivery and turned it upside down. It taught me a step by step system to follow in terms of developing a keynote speech at the highest level. The best part, it introduced me to Steve Siebold. I knew from the moment he walked in and started talking, he was the real deal and that I wanted to be standing in his shoes someday.

Fast forward three years, and I've had the opportunity to speak with Steve around the country and get to know him at a level very few speakers do. Over the past 18 months, I've talked to over 1500 speakers who were trying to take their speaking to the next level. What I've learned from all these conversations is that few speakers understand how this business works. They are talented people with great messages, yet can't figure out how to take it to the next level. It seems as if 99% of them think differently about the business than Steve, yet want to have the kind of success he's had.

One of the most common questions they'd ask me is "How did Steve break into the business and become a million dollar speaker?" It's a great question and one that I thought the speaking world should hear. That's when I went to Steve with the idea for this book. I want every person whose dream it is to become a big time speaker to know his story and learn how he thinks.

What's in this book is the no BS version of the speaking business. If you're seeking the truth on how this business works and what it takes, get ready.

I sincerely hope Steve's story motivates you, as it has me, and that this book assists you on your journey to becoming the next million dollar speaker!

To your success!

Elliot Saltzman

Minneapolis, Minnesota

TABLE OF CONTENTS

STEVE SIEBOLD'S STORY

I was sitting in the green room at FOX studios in Atlanta, waiting to be interviewed via satellite by Stuart Varney in New York on Fox Business Network's Varney & Co. My new book, *Sex, Politics, and Religion: How Delusional Thinking is Destroying America* was grabbing headlines around the world. My dream of becoming a best-selling author, speaker, and thought leader had come true, and I was living a life most people only see in movies—the life of million-dollar homes, luxury cars and limousines, parties at the Playboy mansion, charity dinners at Trump's, and movie premiers in Hollywood. Life was good and getting better with every speech, TV interview, and radio show. Thanks to massive media exposure, in the past three years, I was able to share my Mental Toughness message with over a 100 million people. My vision had become reality.

But how did I get here?

Was it brilliance or blind luck? The truth is neither. We've all heard the saying that when the student is ready, the teacher will appear. That's what happened to me. It's a story that spans nearly twenty-five years, but here's the *Reader's Digest* version:

I grew up in Chicago and competed on the national junior tennis circuit in the 1970s and 80s. My coaches thought I had the talent to make it to the top fifty in the world, but I only made it to the top 500. After sixteen years of four-hour practice days, cross country travel, and sacrifices from my family, I had failed. I was twenty-two-years-old. My dream was over, and I was lost. Since the age of six, I had focused on becoming a professional tennis player, and I wasn't sure how to start living an ordinary life. It was something entirely unfamiliar.

My classes at the University of South Alabama were interesting, but I spent half the time day-dreaming about my next big goal. I didn't know what it was, but I knew one thing for sure: this time I was going to succeed. Competitive tennis had armed me with the greatest skill anyone can possess: mental toughness. I didn't possess the raw intellect to build rockets or cure cancer, but in a battle of pure persistence, I was hard to beat. The key was to match my mental strength with my new vision, and I didn't have a clue how to do it. I spent hours in the library scouring the shelves for areas of interest. I wanted to do something I loved as much as I had loved tennis because my experience taught me that was the only way I would be able to endure the hardship it takes to achieve world-class success. This was the greatest lesson of my childhood, and I knew it would eventually lead to uncommon success. The question was, success in what?

This question plagued me twenty-four hours a day. I had been trained since childhood to block out distractions, compartmentalize my emotions, and focus on the task at hand, and after so many years, I couldn't turn it off. It haunted me. Street entrepreneurs, those without Wharton degrees or wallets full of money, endure enormous amounts of rejection, humiliation, and suffering. My background had given me the necessary tools to thrive in almost anything, and I had the love of my life backing me up. My girlfriend-turned-wife Dawn Andrews was there from the beginning to apply bandages, offer encouragement, and send me back to the front when I was ready to fight again. No one has ever had a bigger fan or stronger support system.

In the fall of 1984, I went to the bank to make a deposit. This guy walked up to me in line at the bank and said, "How would you like to make an extra $5,000 a month?"

Now, keep in mind that this is 1984, and I'm a college student living on ten dollars a week! $5,000 per month in those days was a lot of money, and he's calling it extra-money?

"My name is Randy," he said, "and if you're interested, meet me at this address tonight and I'll give you the details."

I thought it was a scam, but I was free that night and I didn't have anything thing to lose.

The meeting was held at a young woman's tiny apartment. An older gentlemen set up a white marker board and made a presentation. He talked about how in the future people would change jobs every few years, and company loyalty would be a thing of the past. He talked about becoming a millionaire. He talked about being free, being rich enough to do anything you wanted to do, and living life on your own terms. That captured my attention. At the end of the presentation, he said, "The opportunity I just showed you is Amway." I thought to myself, what's Amway?

Dawn attended the next meeting with me, and we signed up as distributors. We spent the next two years going to school and selling Amway products. College was supposed to be our education, but instead it was our entry into entrepreneurship, which turned out to be our real education. The experience taught us basic business skills and gave us a crash course in handling rejection. But the most powerful part of the experience for me was watching the speakers on stage. Their eloquence, stage presence, and sheer intensity left me breathless. I knew someday I wanted to electrify audiences the way they did.

In 1986, Dawn and I married and moved to Bradenton, Florida. I started teaching tennis, and she got a job as a food broker. For the next five years, we worked by day and brainstormed by night.

One morning, in 1991, I was lifting weights in our apartment building exercise room, listening to Tony Robbins talk about dreams, and it finally came to me: I'm going to be an author and professional speaker. I had no idea how to do it, but Tony Robbins said on the tape that I didn't need to know how. I just had to know why.

I knew why.

I had lived a unique experience and learned world-class focus, persistence, and tenacity. Through my writing and speaking, I could teach people these lessons. Just the thought of it kept me up at night. I went home and told Dawn my idea.

"I think you should go for it!" she said. "What do we need to do first?"

"I have no idea!" I said.

For the next two years, I took writing classes at the community center, worked on my writing skills, and read books about the speaking business. Then one day, the phone rang. It was my brother. He was starting a new business, installing industrial machinery, and wanted to know if I was interested in joining him. Moving and installing industrial machinery is what most of my family has done for decades. It's a lucrative business. My brother's offer was appealing, not because of the business, but because of him. I'm the youngest of four boys, and my brothers are six, ten, and eleven years older than I. I worshipped them growing up but was always too young to be part of their inner circle. This was my chance. Here I was, at thirty-years-old, still trying to gain entry into their club. I told my brother I would think about it and called my dad. I've never seen him so excited. My dad grew up in Chicago during the days of Al Capone and the Great Depression and had worked as a bricklayer. This was a guy with classic mid-western, conservative values, to which a hand shake was as good as a contract. When he promised you something, you could take it to the bank.

Mom and Dad's enthusiasm, Dawn's support, and my emotional need to bond with my brothers drove me to make a disastrous decision. I joined the company in 1994 and put my speaking/writing dream on hold. Deep down, I knew it was a mistake. After eighteen months of misery, I had lost all respect for my brothers, and even worse, respect for myself for going into business with people I didn't trust. With Dawn's help and my parents' support, I quit. The lowest point came a few weeks later, when I was standing in the unemployment line with my dad. It was the most depressing day of my life. I had no money, no job, and no home.

Dawn and I considered getting jobs, but as entrepreneurs, we knew better. Once you're bitten by the entrepreneurial bug, there's no going back. We decided that she would go into real estate, and I would start my speaking career. As soon as the business could afford it, she would quit real estate and run my speaking business. We moved into my parents' ten-by-ten spare bedroom and began working eighteen-hour days. Dawn won Palm Beach County, Florida, real estate Rookie of the Year, beating out over 3,000 other realtors. Her organizational genius and world-class work ethic made her a star. Thank God for her early success, because I was failing miserably. I opened a small executive office in Boynton Beach, Florida, and worked seven days a week. I borrowed money on credit cards at 22% interest to hire six different speaking and marketing consultants. I was calling a hundred companies a day pitching my mental toughness speech, with meager results. My self-esteem was in the tank, and I was getting more depressed by the day. Eighteen months earlier I was coaching tennis, building the blueprint of my dream life, and I was happy. Now I was heartbroken over losing my brothers, failing in business, and living in a ten-by-ten room. But Dawn and my parents continued to encourage me. Several times, I asked Dawn whether I should quit the business and go into real estate with her.

"Oh, no," she said. "I know you. You'll be reading books about writing and speaking on the side, daydreaming about what might have been, and figuring a way to go back in business. You'll never be satisfied doing anything else."

Of course she was right, and I felt lucky to be married to someone who knew me so well and was willing to sacrifice for my success. That being said, my depression deepened. This isn't good when you're a mental toughness coach! It took every bit of mental toughness I had to hang on, and the truth is, I wouldn't have had the strength without the support of Dawn and my parents. I wish I could say I was so tough I didn't need anyone, but that would be a lie. I was struggling just to stay in the game. I did the best I could, but lost over $50,000 my first year as a professional speaker. I was speaking at local car dealerships, real estate offices, and anywhere else they would pay me, but it wasn't enough.

And then one particularly gloomy morning, I was sitting in my office trying to figure out what to do, when this guy knocked on my half-open door and said, "Hi! I'm John Spannuth. I have an office down the hall. I just wanted to say hello." His cheerfulness was infectious but irritating because I was so depressed.

"I'm Steve. Nice to meet you." I'm usually pretty friendly, but I wasn't in the mood for small talk.

Unaffected by my lack of enthusiasm, he said, "What kind of work do you do?"

"I'm a writer and professional speaker on mental toughness."

"Wow! That's great! Do you know Bill Gove?"

"Who's Bill Gove?" I said.

"He's the father of professional speaking, and one of the most successful professional speakers of all time. He's a friend of mine. Maybe we can have lunch sometime and I can introduce you."

"Sure, that would be fine. Nice meeting you." I was unimpressed because I had never heard of Bill Gove. I decided to do some research to see if any of the big speakers in the business knew him. I emailed everyone from Jim Cathcart to Ty Boyd, the ten giants of the industry. They didn't know me, but I had been listening to their recordings for years. I got their email addresses from the National Speakers Association directory and hoped they would respond. I left the office that night hoping at least one of them would reply. The next morning I opened my email and couldn't believe my eyes. All ten had responded, and what they wrote stunned me.

Ty Boyd said, "Billy Gove is the master of masters. The best of the best."

Jim Cathcart said, "If you wanted to be a professional hockey player, the greatest mentor you could have would be Wayne Gretzky. Bill Gove is the Wayne Gretzsky of professional speakers."

Don Hutson called him "the patriarch of the speaking business, the great mentor to us all."

The accolades went on and on. The reverence these giants had for Bill Gove was incredible. I jumped out of my office chair and ran down the hall to John Spannuth's office. "How fast can you get me a meeting with Bill Gove?" I said.

"I'll call him right now."

I'm not a big fan of religion, but at that moment I remember praying that Bill Gove was going to be my mentor. I had tears in my eyes when John Spannuth said, "It's all set. Next Wednesday at Mike's Grill on Congress Avenue. It's Bill's favorite restaurant. Bring your camera and something for him to sign. You'll want to get his autograph and a photo."

For the next five days, I did nothing but research Bill Gove. It turned out he had been the first president of the National Speaker's Association back in 1972. His mentor had been Dr. Kenneth McFarland, the dean of American speakers. This lineage of speakers and mentors these men were part of included William Jennings Bryan and Mark Twain. I had tapped into the richest legacy in the professional speaking industry. I was in way over my head.

Bill Gove had been an all-star salesman for companies like Beechnut and 3M and had started speaking in 1945 after seeing Dr. McFarland speak in St. Paul, Minnesota, and persuading him to be his mentor. In 1947, Bill Gove opened his own speech workshop and began passing down the wisdom from the masters who preceded him. The Bill Gove Speech Workshop would eventually become the gold standard of keynote speech training programs, with more million-dollar speaker graduates than any program in history.

The morning before our lunch meeting, I was going stir-crazy sitting in my office. I was so excited that I couldn't concentrate, so I pulled out the National Speakers Association member directory and started flipping through it. I thought to myself, who is the biggest name in this book? And then it hit me: It was Cavett Robert, the founder of the National Speakers Association. He was eighty-nine-years-old, retired, and living in Scottsdale, Arizona. His phone was listed in the directory. I thought, I wonder if he knows Bill Gove? I wonder what he thinks about him. I took a deep breath and dialed the number. An elderly woman answered. I later found out it was Cavett's wife, Trudy.

I said, "May I speak with Cavett?"

Ten seconds later I heard, "This is Cavett Robert."

"Is this THE Cavett Robert, the founder of the National Speakers' Association?"

"Yes, it is."

"Mr. Robert, I'm a new speaker and—"

"Son, I think you have the wrong number. You're probably looking for the National Speakers' Association office."

"No sir, I'm—"

"Son, I'm no longer in the business and can't help you. You'll need to call the NSA office. Best of luck to you."

"Sir, before you hang up I just called to tell you I was having lunch with a friend of yours." (I prayed they were friends.)

"Oh? Who's that?"

"Bill Gove."

It was as if I had hit the secret pass code.

"Well, why didn't you say so in the first place! How is Bill doing?"

"Oh, I think he's doing great, Mr. Robert."

"You know he was our first president. Bill is the man who recruited the original group that became the National Speakers' Association.

There would be no NSA without Bill Gove. He's one of the greatest professional speakers that ever lived."

I could barely speak. I felt like I was in a movie, except this was *really happening.* I said, "I'm thinking about attending the Bill Gove Speech Workshop."

"That's the smartest thing any speaker could do." And I'll never forget what he said next: "Son, any friend of Bill Gove's is a friend of mine. If there's anything I can ever do to help you, you have my number. And please tell Bill I said 'hello.'"

"Thank you, sir. I'll do that." And I hung up.

It was like someone whacked me over the head with a two-by-four. Here I was, a thirty-two-year-old nobody who lost $50,000 my first year in the business, and the founder of the National Speakers' Association just offered to help me. On top of that, in forty-five minutes I was going to meet the man all the top speakers worshipped. I thought to myself, I'm at the lowest point of my life. Could today be the first day of my comeback? Could this be the break I've been working for?

In forty-five minutes, I would have my answer.

John Spannuth knocked on my door and said, "Are you ready to go?"

We got to the restaurant, and Bill and his wife, Ada, were waiting for us by the entrance. John Spannuth, in his most cheerful voice, said, "Steve Siebold, I want you to meet the great Bill Gove!"

I was star-struck. I reached out to shake his hand because I didn't know better. See, no one shook Bill Gove's hand. Bill was a hugger. I would learn later that he was the man who, in the late 1940s, introduced the hug to professional speakers onstage. He called it "the ultimate love gesture." Bill opened his arms, wrapped them around me and said, "I understand you want to be a speaker."

I was a little freaked out. I didn't come from a hugging family, and probably hadn't hugged more than two or three people in my life. I said, "Yes sir. I've been in the business full time for a year.

"How is it going?"

"Terribly."

"We'll see if we can do something about that."

"Yes, sir. That would be great." We sat down for lunch.

Bill said, "Tell me about yourself and your business. Start from the beginning. I want to hear the whole story. I gave him my best ten-minute overview.

"Tell me more, Steve. I need to know as much as possible if I'm going to be able to help."

Not wanting to abuse his good will, I stopped every five minutes or so, and every time I did he would ask me more questions.

Two hours later, he said, "Kid, I think you have a good start. You're smart, motivated, and your take on mental toughness picks up where a lot of speakers leave off. I think you will do just fine."

As soon as got up to leave, Bill's wife, Ada, said, "Would you be interested in attending the Bill Gove Speech Workshop?"

Bill laughed. "She's my manager and best salesperson."

Knowing there was NO WAY I could afford it, I said, "ABSOLUTELY!"

The Monday following our lunch meeting, I spoke for a branch of Coldwell Banker in Delray Beach, Florida, and drove directly from the speech to a tiny motel in West Palm Beach, where Bill held his workshops. In those days, Bill only conducted one-on-one workshops, having tired of coaching groups. The first thing he said was, "Before you give me your speech, I want to ask you a serious question."

"Okay."

"Is there any way I can talk you out of this business?"

I thought he was joking. I laughed. "No, sir! I'm ready to roll!"

"I'm serious, Steve. Because if I can talk you out of it, I need to return your money right now. There are much easier ways to make a living, and if you aren't totally committed to this business, you have no chance of making it. I want you to know upfront that the odds are against you."

Once I realized he was dead serious, my eyes filled with tears. "Mr. Gove, I've been really happy all my life. I won fifty-seven junior tennis titles and was counted among the top 500 players the world. I built one of the most successful private coaching practices in the state of Florida. I have a beautiful wife who is my biggest fan and most loyal supporter. Even when I was losing tennis matches, I always felt like a winner. Two years ago, I made the biggest mistake of my life. I got into business with family I loved but didn't trust and they got the best of me. I've lost everything I own. For the first time in my life, I feel like a loser. I don't want to feel like that anymore."

There was complete silence, for what seemed like forever. "I see," he said. "Are you willing to do everything I tell you?"

"Yes, sir. You say jump, and I say, how high? I'm a good student, Mr. Gove. I've been coached all my life."

"Are you willing to ignore everyone else and only follow me?"

"Yes sir."

"Okay. Give me your speech. Let's see what you've got, kid."

So I did. It was best forty-minute speech of my life. He clapped at the end and smiled.

"How much do you get for that?" I said.

"$500."

"Yeah, that's about what it's worth."

"But Mr. Gove, my dream is to get $5,000 a speech."

"Your ideas on mental toughness are groundbreaking and compelling, and it's obvious that you're a true expert. The problem is you sound like a schoolteacher. Keynote speaking is show business, kid. You're going to have to learn how to entertain an audience."

"But I have no interest in entertaining, Mr. Gove. I want to teach people about mental toughness."

"Steve, you should be a college professor. I think you would be a good one."

"Mr. Gove, I don't even know why I went to college. It was a waste of time. I don't want to be a professor."

"Well, then, we're going to have to teach you how to move from being an informer to a performer. Are you ready to get started?"

"I'm ready, Mr. Gove."

"That's good, kid. Because by the time I'm done with you, you'll be on your way. It's a skill very few people in the world understand, and if you learn it, you can write your own ticket for the rest of your life."

The next two days were spectacular. I was so excited. I was finally on the road to my new life, and now I had a mentor to guide me. Life looked good again. Bill offered me a twelve-month video coaching program after the speech workshop, and I purchased it immediately. Every month I would videotape myself delivering a three to five minute story, and he would critique it. Within six months, I started to understand the Bill Gove System, and I also realized he was a creative genius. I started picking up the subtleties and nuances of the system, and everything he taught me started working. Bill recommended that I pull myself out of the business and focus exclusively on giving two hundred civic club speeches, so I could practice and learn his system. He didn't want the marketplace to see me as a $500 speaker. He wanted me to speak at every Rotary and Kiwanis Club in Florida. So that's what I did for the next thirteen months. When I wasn't speaking at a breakfast, lunch, or dinner, I was rehearsing and writing. I spent eighteen hours a day at my office, sometimes crashing on the couch from sheer exhaustion. One day, the owner of the building knocked on my door and asked me if everyone was okay.

"Sure, why do you ask? Didn't you get my rent check?" I said.

"Yes, I got it. But I've been driving by the building every night for the past few months, and your light is always on. Steve, I don't want to embarrass you, but are you living in the office?"

"No, Bob, but I'm going home at one or two a.m. every night. My business is failing, and I'm trying to save it. I don't know any other way. I can't let it go without a fight." If I only knew then that years later Bob would tell my rags-to-riches story every chance he had. But that day he wished me the best and said he knew what it was like to fight for a dream. He had done it years before and it made him a millionaire. A millionaire, I thought, geez. I just want to pay off my credit cards and move out of my mom and dad's spare bedroom.

After completing two hundred civic club speeches, Bill said I was learning the system faster than anyone he had ever coached, and that put me in some pretty good company. I was pleased, but still flat broke and directionless in the business. I was also emotionally scarred by the destruction of my family. I was walking around like a wounded animal. I was suffering from a broken heart with no time to heal. I woke up every day with a knot in my stomach, but I had to keep moving forward. It was either give up and get a job, or stay tough and work like an animal to break into the business. I had my wife and Mom and Dad behind me, and now I had this genius named Bill Gove, who just happened to be the father of the industry. There was no way I could give up, but in all honesty, there were days when I wanted to. Being broke and broken-hearted is a bad combination, and it was a struggle just to get out of bed every morning.

You're probably thinking: *this guy is a mental toughness coach, and he could barely get out of bed?*

You're right. It doesn't fit. All I can tell you is that at one time I was a fierce competitor at a pretty high level. One of the top players at Harvard University I had competed against for years told me one time that he hyper-ventilated every time we played. He said my intensity scared him. It was probably the best compliment I ever had as a competitor. But those days were gone, and I wasn't feeling tough anymore. I'm not proud of the fact that the dual challenges of financial and emotional hardship almost broke me. All I can say is that everyone has a breaking point, and I was approaching mine. All I wanted was to feel normal again and escape the sick feeling I had in my stomach every day. I had invested thirteen months learning how to deliver a keynote speech to every animal club in Florida, and I was getting closer. I just needed a break. I was sitting in my office at ten p.m. one night, and an idea struck me like a bolt of lightning. I ran down the hall to John Spannuth's office. Luckily, he was working late. I said, "John, I have an idea I need to bounce off you."

John Spannuth is one of the most positive guys I had ever met, and also one of the smartest. He always had my best interests at heart. John said, "Sure, fire away!"

"I'm going to write a business proposal to Bill Gove about creating a partnership. He can teach me the business, and I'll sell seats to his workshop. What do you think?"

"Sensational! Great idea, Steve! Go for it."

I spent the next couple of days writing the proposal and setting up a time to meet with Bill. We met at his country club for breakfast.

"So what did you want me to talk about, kid?" he said.

"Are you happily retired, Bill? What do you do every day?"

"I get up around eight o'clock, go to the club and have breakfast with my friends, hit a few golf balls, and go home for a nap. I'm eighty-four-years-old, and I get tired late in the morning. Then I have lunch and watch the ball game. And unless I'm teaching a speech workshop, that's about it."

"Are you happy doing that?"

"No."

I was stunned. I never expected him to say "no." This was my chance. My chance of a lifetime! "Would you be interested in starting a business with me? Here's my proposal." I slid the ten-page proposal across the breakfast table and held my breath.

He didn't say anything. He just started reading it. It was the longest five minutes of my life. What had started out as a wild idea was now under consideration. Would he laugh at me, or did I actually have a shot at bagging the biggest elephant in the business? I could feel the sweat rolling down my back. I was ready to give him any terms he wanted, and the proposal already stated that I would fund the business with my own money. Of course, I didn't have any money, but that didn't matter. If he said "yes," I would find a way to raise the cash. He read over the main pages of the proposal, removed his glasses, and slid the paper back over to me. I held my breath and waited. It suddenly occurred to me that my fate was in the hands of a man who didn't need me—a living legend who had done it all. He had fame, fortune, and the respect of millions of fans around the world. And I was just a broke thirty-two-year-old kid living in my parent's spare bedroom. All I had to offer this man was my boundless energy and enthusiasm, which would eventually make him richer. But did he need the money? Did he even care about the money? All I could do was pray he did because I had nothing else to offer.

Finally, in what sounded like slow motion, he said, "I'm in."

You could have knocked me over with a feather. I finally took a breath and said, "You're in?" I couldn't believe my ears.

"I'm in on one condition."

"Okay."

"I fund half of the start-up costs. If we're going to be partners, I need to pay my half."

My eyes welled up with tears, but he pretended not to notice. I had just become the business partner of the greatest keynote speaker in the history of the industry and the most successful keynote speaking coach who ever lived. At that moment, I knew my life would be forever changed, and I was so excited I practically ran out of that country club. The first thing I did was call Dawn. She said, "I knew you could do it! This is going to be big!" The next people I called were my Mom and Dad. They were as excited as Dawn. This is the kind of moral support I would get in business from them for the next five years, and it was critical to our success.

Two weeks later, we formed Gove-Siebold Group, opened our office in Florida, and went to work. Our first project was a video album called *Everything You Need to Know about Speaking*, which was me interviewing Bill about the speaking business. The entire project cost $7,500. It was a low budget, one-camera shoot. That's all we could afford without putting our little company in debt, which we agreed not to do. To this day, sixteen years later, Gove-Siebold Group has always been debt-free. It's one of our secrets to success. Larry Wilson, founder of Wilson Learning, was the first to review the album. Bill and Larry spent a week at Larry's home in Grand Cayman dissecting it. I went to pick them up at Miami Airport, walked into the baggage claim, and spotted them across the room. There were at least 500 people between us, and Larry Wilson starts yelling, "Hey, that's Steve

Siebold, the star of the new video! That guy is huge!" I had never met Larry Wilson in my life, but I had read most of his books and knew he was a genius. Now I was witnessing what millions of fans called "The Larry Wilson Magic." He was making me feel like a star. That was my introduction to, and my first encounter with, the great Larry Wilson. Over the years Larry and I would become close friends, and he would teach me how the business worked in a way no one else could. His advice would make us millions. But that day I was overwhelmed by his charisma, humility, and generosity. Five minutes after meeting him, I understood why he was one of the giants of the industry.

The next move we made was to form board of advisors to guide the company and give our start-up company the street credibility we needed. Bill made a list of sixteen of the most successful speakers who were his students. I called all sixteen, and fifteen said, "yes." Zig Ziglar was the only speaker who declined.

For the next three months, I sold the video album, helped Bill run the speech workshop, and spoke everywhere I could, mostly for free.

Then one day, Bill calls me and says, "All right kid. You've been working hard and you're ready for the big stage. Bob Proctor just called and asked me to speak at Roe Bartle Hall in Kansas City for 7,000 salespeople, and you and I are going to do it together."

"We are?"

"Yep, and we need to write the speech and start rehearsing immediately. We only have three months to prepare."

Three months later, a stretch limousine pulls up at the Mulebach Hotel in Kansas City, picks us up, and drives us into the arena, right to the back of the stage. I turned to Bill and asked, "Is this how all of the big speeches are?"

"Yep. After this speech, Steve, your life will never be the same. This is the break you've been working for. Tonight is going to be one of the biggest of your life. I guarantee it."

As usual, he was right. We walked off the stage that night, and people surrounded us like movie stars. We flew into Kansas City with $5,000 in our business account and twenty-four hours later we had $132,000. We had earned $127,000 in a forty-minute keynote speech, and I had just spoken to more people in twelve minutes than I had my entire life. Bill Gove was right: my life was never the same.

Bob Proctor called a few days later, and I thanked him for getting us the speech and helping us to sell so many video albums. Without Bob's help, it never would have happened. Bob said he was happy to do it. "Bill Gove has IOU's spread out all over the world. Congratulations, Mr. Siebold. You're the man who's going to cash them in." Bob Proctor would turn out to be instrumental in our success. He sent us hundreds of referrals and to this day has refused to take a penny. He's been our single biggest promoter and friend.

After Kansas City, we were invited by Bob and many of his clients to speak all over the country and around the world. We did programs in Europe, Australia, Scandinavia, Canada, and in almost every state in the U.S. At one point we were speaking to 10,000 people per week. Any audience under 5,000 looked small. It was amazing. Bill and I created new products, programs, and speeches. We conducted the Bill Gove Speech Workshop across the country for the next five years. In early 2001, we hired Dawn to run the company, so we could focus on speaking and writing. We made a lot of money and had a lot of fun.

Being on the road with Bill for five years was the time of my life. He taught me every detail of the business from the bottom up, and whatever he didn't excel in, he connected me with people who did. Larry Wilson flew Dawn and me to his Lake Minnetonka mansion and spent ten days teaching us how to build a seven-figure speaking, training, and consulting business. Bill Brooks taught me how to break into big companies and use vertical and horizontal marketing. Bob Proctor made me a millionaire by teaching me how to think like one. There were many others too numerous to mention, and they all treated me like Bill Gove's kid. As Bob Proctor said to me one day, I now had an Ivy League education in the speaking business. Bob said, "Steve, you have the single best speaker's education of anyone in this business."

Bill got sick in the summer of 2001 and we contacted every doctor in our reach to save him. He was eighty-nine-years-old, and still one of the highest-paid speakers alive. The last speech we delivered was for Bob Proctor's 3% club on September 25, 2001. A few weeks later, Bill and I were honored by President George W. Bush, to serve on the 9/11 charity awards committee in Washington, DC, along with Doug Wead, Merv Griffin, Cheryl Ladd, Pat Boone, and a host of other movie stars and celebrities. We were scheduled to share the stage with the president in Washington on December 10, 2001. Bill Gove died on December 9, just one month shy of his ninetieth birthday.

In July 2002 in Orlando, Florida, 250 of the biggest speakers in the business gathered to celebrate the life of Bill Gove. It was an extraordinary event.

Dawn and I continued to build the Gove-Siebold Group. In 2005, I wrote my first book, *177 Mental Toughness Secrets of the World-Class*, which went on to sell over 100,000 copies around the world. My fan base and income exploded almost overnight. From 2005 to 2012, I wrote four more books, sold millions of dollars in speeches, training, and consulting, and appeared on hundreds of radio and television shows. In 2011, the National Speakers' Association named me the 2011 Chairman of the Million Dollar Speakers Group, arguably the most prestigious and powerful group of millionaire professional speakers in the world. Our business is on track to double again in 2013, and the future looks better than ever.

And that's my story.

Now the question is; what's yours? I'm guessing that the reason you purchased this book is that you and I share the same dream, the speaker's dream. It's the greatest dream in the world, and the only question is, can you make it come true?

Look, I'm not sure how bad you want this and I have no crystal ball. But let me leave you with this: if you can't imagine doing anything else with your life and you have the heart of a lion, you have a real shot at making it big in this business. The odds are against you, but isn't that true of every big dream? Study this book like a scientist. Read it over with a yellow highlighter and absorb every word as if your life depends on it. Elliott Saltzman did a wonderful job drilling down on every conceivable question about this business. The extensive interview you're about to read was conducted over eight months, and the level of detail about what it takes to make it is unparalleled in this business. Elliot refused to stop until I unveiled the good, bad, and ugly of this industry. I'm not overstating it by saying the information in this book could make your career.

I wish you the very best in your quest to make your speakers dream a reality. You and I are kindred spirits, and even though we haven't met, I'll be secretly cheering you on from the sidelines.

Now you know my story. It's time to create yours.

STATE OF THE SPEAKING BUSINESS

 How would you describe the current state of the speaking business?

 It's in free fall and speakers are going out of business every day. The supply of speakers is going down, yet the demand is going up. This is the best time in the sixty-year history of the business to get started.

 Has it been affected by the recession?

 Severely. The good news is it's weeding out the mediocre speakers and creating opportunity for new speakers.

 It seems as if there are more problems than ever in both the public and corporate market. Has this caused a significant demand for speakers?

 Yes, but they're looking for thought leaders who can solve problems.

What do you mean by "thought leaders"?

People with new ideas who solve problems.

How has the business changed since you started?

It was flooded with people like me trying to break in. Now many speakers have gone broke, and the newer speakers think companies aren't hiring. The fact is that companies need us more than ever. Corporate America is sitting on $2.5 trillion dollars in cash because they are paralyzed with fear. They're operating in uncharted waters, and they're desperate for answers. This is the opportunity of a lifetime for speakers with solutions.

Do you have to sell yourself differently today than you did in the past?

You have to be better at everything, including the sales process. That's why we started the Corporate Speaker Sales School, where we have corporate executives teaching speakers how to sell them.

Do you think it's easier or harder for speakers to break into the business now?

Both. There's more opportunity, but you have to be better than before the crash. The mediocre speakers regurgitating The Secret and Think and Grow Rich are going out of business, but the thought leaders are thriving. I think this will continue well into the future, and it's a very positive thing. The speaking business is coming of age, and I'm more excited about it than ever.

What do speakers have to do differently?

They have to be better at every aspect of the business, especially on stage and in their ability to offer unique solutions their clients can't see themselves.

In late 2012, when most speakers were closing their doors after years of being in the business, what was the feeling among the million dollar speakers at the National Speakers' Association meeting in Indianapolis?

Total optimism and excitement. We all agreed the business was changing, but for the better. Many of these speakers got richer during the recession.

Which market was hit harder: public or corporate?

Probably the public market, because corporations are still rich and the general public is broke.

Do you have to decrease your fees during tough times?

Some speakers did. I decided not to. And luckily business has been good through the recession.

So corporations are still hiring?

Yes.

What are executives saying?

They need help. Positive-thinking platitudes aren't enough. They are looking for smart people to solve problems.

What kind of speakers are they hiring?

 Thought leaders with specific solutions.

 Are there certain topics they're looking for more than others in today's market?

 Everything they were hiring us for before the crash, minus the fluff speakers repeating worn-out messages.

 Are there certain topics that will be hotter in the future?

 Technology is a hot topic and will continue to grow.

 Does it seem as if the professional speaking business has become more or less popular than it was in the past?

 More popular and profitable for a smaller group of speakers. The middle class of the speaking business is dead, and it's the best thing that's ever happened to this industry.

Are there any statistics on how many people try to break into the business every year?

I've always heard that about 50,000 people attempt to break into the business every year.

How many do you think actually succeed?

Very few.

Is this number going up or down?

The percentage of people who succeed is going down. That's why you see the same speakers dominating every year.

That goes against what many speaker trainers are telling aspiring speakers.

Telling speakers what they want to hear instead of the truth is very profitable. It's unethical but profitable. We tell people the truth so they know what they're getting themselves into. It's the right thing to do.

What would you compare it to? Trying to break into Hollywood, becoming a professional athlete, or becoming a doctor or lawyer?

You have a far better chance of becoming a doctor or lawyer. It's closer to moving to Hollywood and trying to break into movies. I mean, honestly, how many people do you know who earn $10,000-20,000 an hour? I'm not talking about celebrities. I'm talking about regular people. Do you know how good you have to be at something to charge $10,000 for an hour of your time? Yet new speakers are fooled into believing they are going to simply hang a shingle and companies are going to beat a path to their door when they have no training or experience in our business. It's delusional. That being said, anyone who knows what they are doing has a shot, but they must be trained professionals who know what they're doing on and off stage. Otherwise, it's just a pipedream.

Are there more people training speakers today than there were in the past?

There seem to be. It's easier to teach someone how to do something than it is to do it. That's why you want to learn from a speaker who is currently near the top of this industry. They are the only people who truly understand the way this business works.

There is a lot of misinformation out there about the speaking business.

Sexy misinformation that tells people what they want hear is profitable.

Have you seen the business change as technology advances?

Yes, and it's fantastic! Video blogs, Facebook, Twitter, and the rest are making it easier for speakers to spread their message. It's all very exciting.

Is it making it easier or tougher for speakers?

If you're good, it makes it easier, and if you're not, it makes you fail faster.

Where do you see the speaking business going as technology keeps advancing?

I think it will continue to create more and more opportunities to share our messages around the world.

Do you think there will be less of a need for speakers in the future? Will speeches turn into events you can watch online?

I think there will be less of a need for speaker's content and more of a need for thought leaders who speak. The former will become a commodity and the latter will continue to be the richest speakers in the business.

It seems as if most of the big name speakers people talk about are getting old. Is there a new generation of speakers replacing them?

Not fast enough. So many of the greats are gone, and the newer generation of speakers seems to lack the platform skills of the legends. That being said, there are some talented young speakers out there doing fabulous work.

It seems as if with all the baby-boomers retiring, the speaking business would see an increase in speakers.

I think we will see an increase in people attempting to break in, but only a few will be good enough to make the cut.

I don't know of any statistics out there, but if you had to guess, what age would you say the average speaker is when they try to break into the business?

I would say between fifty and sixty years of age. The older you are in this business, the more credibility you have. I lost a national convention keynote a few years ago to Charlie Tremendous Jones, who was eighty-seven-years-old at the time. When every other industry puts sixty-five-, seventy-five-, and eighty-five-year-olds out to pasture, our industry celebrates and embraces their experience and wisdom. I know speakers that started in their eighties. Gray hair is a saleable asset in this industry.

Is the business dominated by men or women?

It's been dominated by men in the past, but more women are going to the top than ever before. Speakers like Jeanne Robertson, Roxanne Emmerich, and Diana Booher are three of the best and brightest in this business. I think women will eventually dominate this industry, and I'm excited about it. Strong female speakers offer a unique perspective.

Is there an advantage for one sex or the other?

I don't think so.

Can you be too young or too old to break in?

Not really. It's more about the solutions you offer and the skills you possess. Age isn't really that important, but I do think audiences embrace older speakers more than our younger counterparts.

It seems like the perception to the buyer is the older you are, the wiser you are. Do speakers who are older typically make more money in the business?

Not necessarily.

It seems as if the newest generation of young speakers who are most well-known have become bigger by teaching people how to speak. Are there very many young million-dollar speakers speaking to corporations?

No. I believe Jason Forrest and Rory Vaden are the youngest members. The average age of the Million-Dollar Speakers Group is probably close to sixty.

It seems as if speakers who've been in business for years are shutting their doors. Why is this?

They were unable to adapt to the changes in the industry, specifically those involving technology. Another major cause of failure during the recession is speakers who are delivering very basic motivational messages that companies are no longer hiring them to deliver. The days of the fluff speaker are gone.

What are the million-dollar speakers doing differently to keep their doors open?

They are delivering the same bleeding edge thought leadership they've always delivered, but they are finding new ways to deliver it. Their ideas have stood the test of the worst economy in the history of the industry. It's pretty impressive.

How many years does it typically take a speaker to break into the business?

Five to seven years if they are creating their own content, one to two years if they license a proven program and learn to sell and deliver it.

Do you see this increasing, decreasing, or staying about the same with today's marketplace?

I think it will stay about the same.

With the advancement in social media, I'd imagine it's a lot easier for speakers today to build a fan base. Has that proven true?

In theory, yes, but only if they are offering a unique point of view that a large group of people sees as different and valuable.

Are speakers, on average, making more or less today than they were in the past?

Much more. In the days of Bill Gove, Cavett Robert, and Zig Ziglar, speakers did well. Today, all the top speakers are multimillionaires.

It seems as if many speakers are speaking abroad. Has the market abroad been affected as much as it has in the U.S.?

Definitely. The recession has been global.

Is the U.S.A. the biggest market for speakers?

The largest and the highest paying.

Is the speaking business becoming bigger in other countries?

Yes. Countries like Germany, Australia, England, and Canada are coming on strong, as are a host of others.

That's exciting for people who want to travel around the world speaking.

Yes it is, and many speakers do.

What speakers will struggle in the future?

The commodity speakers will always struggle. The speakers spewing age-old positive thinking platitudes will struggle. The speakers who think content is king will struggle. The thought followers will struggle.

What will speakers have to get better at in the future?

They will have to be more entertaining and exciting than ever. In the age of audiences with smart phones, we can't afford to lose their attention for a second. Platform skills and excellent speech writing will make or break keynote speakers even more in the future than they do now.

Have you noticed audiences getting tougher now that everyone has a telephone in their lap during a speech?

Absolutely. It's a huge issue.

Who will be successful in the future?

Speakers, who can simultaneously entertain, educate, and lead an audience down a linear path. It's a tall order, and it takes training to be successful.

Any other thoughts on the future of the business?

It's all very exciting. The future of this business belongs to the competent thought leader operating on the bleeding edge of progressive ideas. The smartest speakers will continue to be the richest and most successful. If you're a serious expert or you're committed to becoming one, your future in this business is unlimited. I believe we will see speakers who become billionaires in this business in the next 20 years. There is so much to look forward to.

SUMMARY

The average speaker I talk to who is about to invest his or her time, money, and energy into pursing their dream of becoming a speaker, almost always wants me to reassure them that there is a market for speakers. They're nervous that with a tough economy and companies cutting budgets that this is a lousy time to pursue a speaking career. For the speakers who are regurgitating the same old messages of positive thinking and goal setting, it is. But for the thought leaders who have a solution to a problem, this is one of the best times ever to break into this business. Corporations have more problems now than ever and are searching for people to solve them.

Based on the conversations I've had with the speakers over the past year, I predict the speaking business is about to explode. Every day it seems as if I'm talking to someone who has recently retired and is searching for something new. 10,000 baby boomers will be retiring every day for the next nineteen years. This generation has the experience and solutions to solve many of the problems facing organizations. As Steve noted in this chapter, the older you are, the more credible you are. I think speaking will be a natural fit for a generation looking for something new to do.

While I predict there will be a surge of new speakers, I do not suggest that there will be a surge of people joining the Million-Dollar Speaker group. In fact, I think there will continue to be only a handful of speakers every decade who go on to become million-dollar speakers. It's not due to lack of talent. I've spoken with speakers over the past year who are extremely talented. In fact, I wouldn't be surprised if some were even more talented than Steve. I predict the trend of only a select few making it to the million-dollar mark will continue since very few have the patience, training, and discipline to do what it takes to make it to the highest level.

TOPICS THAT SELL

 What topic do you speak on?

 Mental toughness.

 How did you come up with it?

 I was a professional tennis player and was trained in mental toughness.

 Did it take you a long time to decide on the topic?

 No, it was the only topic I ever considered.

Were other speakers speaking on Mental toughness, or were you the first one?

There were others, but they didn't have the same philosophy or approach that I did.

How much time do you spend studying mental toughness?

About two hours a day.

Should a speaker choose a topic based on how many people are already speaking on it?

Absolutely not. They should select a topic about which they have expertise and passion.

It's a pretty big deal choosing your topic. Do most speakers stick with a topic or do they change it if they get bored?

Changing topics is dangerous. When companies are paying big money for an expert who speaks, they lose confidence in someone who changes topics. Doctors don't change specialties. Neither do attorneys. Speakers should learn by their example.

What other topics do you speak on?

 None.

 Do most speakers speak on more than one topic?

 Yes, and it's one of the reasons they earn so little money.

 Does it position you differently if you speak on more than one?

 Yes, it positions you as a jack-of-all-trades and an expert in none.

 You have been interviewed on the Golf Channel about Tiger Woods, on "Good Morning, America" about weight loss, and on Fox Business Network about money. Aren't you speaking on different topics?

 No. Everything I speak about is mental toughness—mental toughness for weight loss, money, and winning in sports.

It's all mental toughness. I just apply it to different areas of life.

It seems as if when most people think of a speaker, they think of a motivational speaker. Do you consider yourself a motivational speaker?

All of us should be motivational. But in general, no, I don't consider myself a motivational speaker. Les Brown and Zig Ziglar are motivational speakers. I'm a mental toughness speaker.

I hear many speakers describe themselves as motivational and inspirational speakers. Are these two different topics?

Not technically, but some speakers would disagree. Motivational speakers, like Les Brown or the late Keith Harrell, pump people up and motivate them to action. Inspirational speakers tell you their story of how they climbed Mount Everest or built a business as a blind person. Their message is: if I can succeed, what's your excuse?

Is mental toughness more of a public or corporate market topic?

Both.

Do some topics limit you to one market or another?

 Yes.

 Give an example.

 Customer service, team building, and leadership are mostly corporate topics. Wealth building, self-esteem and relationships are public market topics

 Is it good to come up with a topic that works in both?

 It gives you more potential income streams.

 It seems as if a lot of people talk about the law of attraction since the hit movie The Secret came out. Can you talk about the law of attraction in corporate America?

 You might speak about it, as a small part of your program, but corporations tends to respond to points with proof, data, and studies. The law of attraction is a nice idea but there is no evidence to support it.

What topics sell?

 Many topics sell. It's more about the speaker and his or her solutions than the topic.

 What are the hot topics right now?

 The ones that solve the biggest problems the clients are currently experiencing. It changes all the time.

 Would you recommend a speaker choose his or her topic based on if it's hot or not?

 No, I'd recommend they choose their topic based on their expertise, credibility and passion.

 Are there certain topics you make more money with?

 The topics that solve the biggest problems pay the most money.

Why?

 They're more valuable to the client.

 Give some examples.

 A company is sued for sexual harassment by an employee and pays millions in a settlement. A world-class expert in how to avoid this in the future would be very highly paid.

 Do you ever get asked to speak to groups on other topics?

 Almost every day.

 Do you take the engagements?

 No.

Why not?

I'm not an expert in anything but mental toughness and critical thinking.

It seems as if the thing that holds back most speakers at the beginning is their topic.

You're right, but it shouldn't. What they should be focused on is building their keynote and getting good on the platform. That's the most important thing and usually gets the least amount of attention with new speakers. Many of them think they are better than they actually are and believe all they need is marketing. It's the biggest reason most new speakers fail. They see a professional speaker and fool themselves into believing they are just as skilled. It's easy to delude yourself when you're new in the business. When Tiger Woods hits a golf ball, he makes it look easy, but when you try to duplicate it, you see how difficult it is. Great speakers make something difficult look easy.

Can a speaker start working in this business before they have a topic, or is the topic the first thing they need to figure out?

They need a program to sell, so the answer is yes, but they should build the keynote first.

How can a speaker get going before they have their topic?

 The first step is getting professional training in keynote speaking. The next step is building a keynote. After that, you select a topic that matches your background, passion, and expertise.

 So a speaker could be building their keynote and have a majority of it done before they have their topic figured out?

 Yes.

 Why don't more people do this?

 Because they confuse public speaking and linear speech writing with professional speaking and non-linear speech writing. Speaking as a hobby is very different than speaking for money. If it were so easy, every college professor, Toastmasters champion, and corporate executive who enters the speaking business would succeed. The fact is that very few of them do because they don't understand the business.

Do you recommend people choose a topic in their field? For example, would you recommend a medical doctor speak to sales teams? Or a sales manager speak to doctors?

The closer you stick to your background, credibility, and expertise, the better the odds you will succeed.

What makes someone an authority on their topic?

Experience, background, education, study, etc.

I hear a lot of people throw around the word "expert." Are you an expert on mental toughness?

I'm an expert on my brand of Mental Toughness. I'm an expert on the system I created, and that's what I sell and deliver.

What does the word "expert" mean to you?

A person with extensive knowledge, experience, and success in a prescribed area.

Is there a certain amount of credibility a person needs to be considered an expert?

 Yes, but as a speaker, results trump everything.

 When people are choosing their topic, should it be broad, like mental toughness, attitude, or motivation, or more specific like communication for managers?

 The more specialized the better, but you also want to make your moniker broad enough to evolve into.

 Any other advice on helping speakers develop their topics?

 Don't pick a topic you don't love, because you're going to speak, write, and be interviewed about it for the rest of your life. Don't sell out your passion. Choose a topic you're excited about and can imagine studying and teaching for the rest of your life.

SUMMARY

Choosing a topic seems to be challenging for many aspiring speakers. As a result, they make the mistake of marketing themselves as a speaker who speaks on several different topics. The problem with this is that it positions them as a commodity speaker. Here's an example to illustrate my point:

I was in the hospital for eight days in the fall of 2011 with pericarditis (inflammation of the pericardium around the heart). Now, imagine I were going to interview two different doctors to decide who would perform heart surgery on me.

The first one says, "Elliot, I do 30 of these operations a year. I also perform knee surgeries, and I'm a general physician who sees patients all day long. I'm a great doctor and I'll do a great job on you."

Then the second doctor comes in and says, "Elliot, I'm a heart surgeon."

"What else do you do?"

"That's it," he says. "I operate on hearts all day long."

Clearly, I'm going to go with the second doctor. But, for some reason, in the speaking business, speakers don't market themselves this way. They market themselves like the first doctor and say, "I'm a speaker, who speaks on sales, leadership, motivation, and marketing." The problem with this is that in the eyes of the buyer, there's no way they can be a world-class authority on all four subjects.

Invest the necessary time selecting your topic and choose one that is broad enough to cover several subjects. For example, Steve speaks on mental toughness. He helps Fortune 500 sales teams increase sales through mental toughness. At the same time, he speaks to the public market about money, weight loss, and relationships. He has even been interviewed around the world on Tiger Woods performance as he's struggled in recent years. While these are a broad group of subjects, they all fall underneath the umbrella of his expertise, which is mental toughness.

In selecting your topic, don't pigeon-hole yourself. If I ask, about what do you speak, you should be able to answer with some type of mantra of five words or fewer. When I spoke at colleges about dating, I created a program called "Will you go out with me?" If I had positioned myself in this way, I would have become pigeon-holed as a dating speaker in the college market. If I had come up with an umbrella topic like communication, I could have been known as a communication speaker with one of the subjects being dating.

Know that if you're struggling to select a topic, you're not alone. It's a completely normal part of the process. Don't feel like you can't move forward in this business without it. The system Steve and many of the top keynoters use to write their speeches grants them the flexibility to insert or change their topic at any time. Learn the system and start writing your keynote. By the time you have thirty minutes of tested material; you'll be able to insert your topic and will have saved yourself six months to six years.

MARKETS

 What are the different markets to speak to?

 The two major markets are public and corporate. The minor market is the association market.

 How do you tell the difference?

 The market is defined by who pays the fee. The public buys tickets while corporations and associations pay speaking fees.

 Is one better than the other?

 The corporate market is the largest and richest. The public market has the biggest audiences, and the association market has audiences full of potential customers. All three have their advantages.

Is one tougher than the others?

 The corporate market is the toughest and most sophisticated. Executives have high expectations of speakers.

 Can you work them all?

 Yes.

 Which market did you start in?

 The public market.

 Why the public?

 It's the easiest and where I got my first break.

Is it a fun market to speak to?

Absolutely!

What's the average public market audience like?

They love personal development and genuinely want to improve their lives. They'll take notes, ask questions, and want your autograph. Speakers become rock stars in the public market.

What size crowds were you speaking to?

My average audience was about 5,000 people but went as high as 20,000.

Were you making more money in the public market from your fees or from the back-of-the-room sales?

Usually Bill Gove (my late business partner and mentor) and I made more from the back-of-room sales. The larger the audience, the more you make.

Can you make a lot of money in the public market?

 Yes.

 Why did you decide to transition to the corporate market?

 Keynote speaking at national conventions for Fortune 500 companies is the major league of the business. I wanted to see if I had what it took to compete with the biggest and best speakers in the world.

 Was it an easy transition?

 No. I was used to speaking to huge crowds, signing autographs, shaking hands and taking pictures. I was a millionaire in the business before I ever gave a corporate speech. It was a humbling experience. I thought I was good but the corporate market pushed me to the next level.

Are the corporate market audiences different?

Yes. Corporate audiences are more discerning and will openly challenge you. They are smart, educated, and savvy, and they don't see you as a rock star. To them, you're just another big mouth with a book.

What were they like?

Tough at best, indifferent at worst.

Which market do you enjoy most?

I love the public market for their passion and enthusiasm and the corporate market for their sophistication and expertise. I don't work in the association market very often because they usually request a discount on your fee from 30%-50%.

What are the pros and cons of the public and corporate market?

People who attend public market programs are the most fun, but they usually have little money to spend on back of room programs. The corporate market audiences are educated and smart, but many of them are overly impressed with their limited level of success and don't understand that they are grossly underselling their services for the perceived security of a regular paycheck.

If you're great in the public market, does that mean you'll be great in corporate and vice versa?

Absolutely not. The corporate market is much more discerning and demanding.

Why did you choose to work with Fortune 500 sales teams?

I love the challenge.

Why have you focused on the pharmaceuticals and financial services industry?

At first, I chose these two because they are the richest industries in business and are easily capable of paying world-class fees. Along the way, I fell in love with both industries for the value they bring to the marketplace. The pharmaceutical industry is demonized in America when they should be celebrated. I've spoken, trained, and consulted thousands of their managers and salespeople, and they are the best of the best. Financial service professionals are dedicated to helping people navigate the markets to secure their future. It's important work done by smart people.

Do you need more credibility to speak to the corporate market?

Yes. The bigger the company, the pickier they are. They can afford to hire anyone they want, and what they want is the best of the best.

What do you need in order to speak to the corporate market?

World-class speaking skills, problem-solving content, and industry credibility.

Which market gives you more rock star status?

 The public market

 Do you position your topic differently in each market?

 To some degree. The public market responds to financial success because their biggest problem is money. The corporate market responds to problem-solving ideas because they have so many problems. If you work both markets, you have to be careful not to mix the two.

 Do you sell yourself differently to each market?

 Oh, yes. They buy very differently.

When I was about to speak to universities, you warned me that the way I was positioning myself, I would get pigeon-holed as a college speaker. Is this common? Do speakers get pigeon-holed into a specific market?

All the time. Most speakers start in the public market and think the corporate market is the same. The truth is it's the difference between college and professional sports: if you're one of the best athletes in college, the pros aren't too big of a leap. But if you're the average college athlete, the pros will eat your lunch. Most speakers test the corporate market and fail, and then spend the rest of their careers in the public market.

For someone like yourself who has never held a corporate job, do you get resistance from audiences and executives who question your credibility?

No, because I sell results.

If you've been a successful corporate executive or employee, will you automatically have an advantage of being a successful corporate speaker?

Absolutely.

What are your thoughts on starting out speaking internally in a company?

 Lots of speakers start this way. It's a good place to begin, but you have to be careful not to fall into the trap of believing just because you can speak to your employees or colleagues that you are good enough to be paid. Public speaking is one thing; professional speaking is another.

 Is that what Bill Gove did at 3M?

 Yeah, he started out speaking internally at 3M but quickly moved on to the local service clubs in the Twin Cities. Then, he began speaking to 3M's customers and eventually the biggest conventions in the country.

 It seems like a lot of talented people speak for free internally and get great reviews. Is it easy to transition out and speak for a fee?

 No, the transition is equivalent to a good weekend golfer deciding to join the PGA tour. Keynote speaking for $10,000-20,000 an hour comes with very high expectations. Most corporate executives are good speakers who can deliver a message minus distractions, but entertaining an audience for 40 minutes requires an entirely differently level of skill and expertise.

Do most of the million-dollar speakers speak to the public or corporate market?

It's a mix, but more of the top speakers focus on the corporate market.

You are one of the top speakers in the world, yet I've talked to people who have never heard of you. Are corporate speakers less well-known?

Yes. Most of the highest-grossing corporate speakers are not well known. They serve niche markets, earn millions of dollars, and can walk down the street unnoticed. Top public market speakers address larger audiences and become more well-known to the personal development industry. Many speakers who are well known to other speakers are also heavily involved in groups like the National Speakers' Association

Which market do you enjoy most?

I enjoy both, but if I had to choose, I would work the corporate market.

Any other advice for speakers on speaking to the different markets?

 Yes. If you believe you have the platform skills and content to speak in the corporate market, I would highly recommend it. But don't make the mistake of winning a Toastmasters contest, speaking as an executive, or speaking in the public market, and think you're going to cruise into the big leagues. Get professional training and give yourself a fighting chance or you're going to get your head handed to you. I know dozens of Fortune 500 executives who have done this, and they have all failed in this business. Keynote speaking for a world-class fee is far more difficult than it looks. In the public market, learn how to layer-sell to maximize your back-of-room sales.

SUMMARY

Generally, most speakers I've talked to haven't put much thought into the different markets to speak to. They're passionate about spreading their message and sincerely believe it will help whoever hears it. This is great; however, many speakers think all audiences are the same. They're not. It's important to know which market you're speaking to so you know how to position yourself. More importantly, it's important to know so you can follow the money. In the speaking business, you have to position yourself very differently with each market. You need to know who it is you want to speak to so you know how to position yourself. A majority of speakers I talk to have the dream of being a million-dollar speaker, yet want to speak to audiences and markets that don't have any money. For example, a speaker will say he wants to speak to parents of student athletes. My question to him is how much money do you want to make? If he says he wants to be a million-dollar speaker and rock star in this business, I ask, "How do you plan to do it?" Speaking to parents, for example, is a public market group. If a speaker wants to command high fees, he needs to wonder how many parents get together in groups and have money to hire a speaker to come talk to them. It doesn't seem likely that there are groups of parents with a large budget to hire a speaker. Of course, the speaker could speak for free and sell a product in the back of the room.

In no way am I suggesting a speaker give up on his passion, sell out for the money, and speak to a market in which he's not interested. That being said, my suggestion would be to consider about what he wants to speak to that group of parents? As I continue asking questions, I determine what really drives the speaker is his passion for support systems. Now imagine what this does to the speaker who positions himself as an authority on support systems. Now this speaker is not limited to any one group or market. This speaker can take his message of support systems to the public or corporate market.

PERSONALITY VS.

COMMODITY SPEAKERS

In the Bill Gove Speech Workshop and FreeSpeakingCourse. com, you make the distinction between a commodity speaker and a personality speaker. Can you talk a little about that?

This is a critical distinction every speaker needs to understand if they want to make serious money in the business. The commodity speaker is hired by topic and price. A company decides to hire a speaker for their meeting or convention, and if they don't have someone who has been referred to them, they'll often go on Google and search for a topical expert they like for the lowest price. Or they'll call a speakers' bureau and book the speaker through them. 90% of the speakers in our business are commodity speakers earning less than $75,000 per year.

And the personality speaker?

The personality speaker is hired for who they are, almost always by referral from another executive. Senior executives aren't fond of trusting the choice of a speaker to a meeting planner. They often want a referral from another senior executive they trust.

That's a pretty general statement.

It is, but in my experience and the experience of most of my speaker friends who are top keynoters, this is what clients tell us. The keynote speaker at a national convention plays a significant role in the success of the meeting, and high-level corporate executives tend to trust their counterparts' referrals over everyone else.

Say more about how you define a personality speaker.

Personality speakers are thought leaders. Executives and companies want to know what they think about their problems and how their unique expertise might help solve them.

Don't commodity speakers have expertise?

Of course, but it's mostly topical expertise. They're like teachers who have studied a subject for years and can repeat what they've learned and impart that knowledge to others.

And that's bad?

It's not bad. It's just not worth much in the marketplace because millions of people can do it. It's a simple case of supply-and-demand, and commodity speakers are in tremendous supply with limited demand.

And the personality speaker?

They are one-of-a-kind because each one of them offers a different interpretation of the content they deliver and the problems of the organization to which they deliver it.

Is there anything else that creates a personality speaker?

Unique delivery style. They're like an original work of art. Some people love them, others hate them, but the bottom line is that no one else is like them. So even with a small fan base in a niche market these speakers can become wealthy.

Commodity speakers earn less than $75,000. What do personality speakers earn?

A million dollars a year or more.

Can you give us an example of a personality speaker?

Tony Robbins is a great example. He's made a fortune being a one-off original. Speakers around the world have attempted to copy him and all have failed.

Anyone else?

Oh, sure. There are hundreds of them. Bob Proctor is one. Larry Wilson is another. Bill Gove was not only a personality speaker, but he taught more people how to become personality speakers than anyone in history. Keith Harrell was a great personality speaker. So were Charles Tremendous Jones, Jim Rohn, and Bill Brooks.

If personality speakers own the majority of the money in the business, why don't most speakers cross over from commodity to personality?

It's not as easy as it sounds.

But you did it.

 I was lucky because I had Bill Gove and his millionaire students guiding my every move. All I had to do was follow the yellow brick road.

 Give us an example of how Bill or one of his students guided you.

 Okay, Larry Wilson was nice enough to invite me to speak at a five-day seminar he was conducting in Minneapolis for Miller Brewing in 1997. I asked Larry how much he was going to make on the deal, and he said his pay for the five days was $100,000.

I almost had a heart attack! I said, "They pay you that much money to deliver the content?"

And Larry said something that changed my entire view of the speaking business. "Steve, at the highest levels of this business, they don't pay for the content. They pay for your personal interpretation of the content."

I swear to God I almost fell out of my chair. To this day, it was one of the wisest, most accurate statements I've ever heard a top speaker make.

How does one's personal interpretation of the content differ from the content itself?

Good question. Let me explain. My topic is mental toughness. By definition, mental toughness is being tough minded and unemotional, especially under pressure. Any sports psychologist will tell you that. My interpretation of mental toughness is different. To me, mental toughness is about controlling your thoughts and emotions to help you get what you want. It's about critical thinking and operating from objective reality as opposed to subjective reality or delusional thinking. It's about thinking for yourself and living life on your own terms. It's about taking responsibility for every action you take and every result you get.

You sound like an evangelist!

I am an evangelist! I'm an evangelist in the church of mental toughness. It's a skill that changes people's lives if they can handle the heat.

What's the heat?

Looking at yourself through an objective, emotionless lens and identifying your true strengths and weaknesses.

Why is that so tough?

Because you begin to see yourself as others see you, from their perspective instead of yours. Sometimes, people don't like what they see.

It seems like it takes five to seven years for a speaker to break into this business. Is that how long it takes to become a personality speaker or can you do it right off the bat?

You can certainly start positioning yourself as a personality speaker from the beginning. Most people don't do it because they don't know how.

How does someone know when they've become a personality speaker?

When clients and companies start asking for them by name instead of by topic or price.

Is it really determined by the money?

Yes and no. Yes, personality speakers are one-off originals, and as a result, they are able to command much higher fees than commodity speakers. No, in the sense that money doesn't determine who is a personality speaker. In other words, if all it took to become a personality speaker was to have high speaking fees, anyone could just raise their fees and they would be there. You become a personality speaker when the marketplace sees you, your point of view, and speaking style as unique and valuable. They don't believe anyone but you can help them solve their problem, so they want you and only you, regardless of your price.

What about a Toastmaster world champion?

I think they're fantastic. The problem is companies don't pay for the speaking style that wins Toastmasters' contests. Companies have problems and they are looking for speakers who can help them. Dramatic award-winning delivery belongs in the church, colleges, and in Toastmasters, not at corporate conventions.

Are you suggesting it's less about the talent and more about the positioning a speaker has in the marketplace?

Talent is a factor in what level market the speaker will be able to serve, but speaking skills are more important for overall success in the business. Positioning and marketing are both important, but you have to have the goods in this business to make it. You can't market your way to the top. Once you get in front of a live audience, it's just you and them. And if you haven't been trained in how to hold their attention, you're dead. No amount of slick marketing will save you. You cannot fake your way to success in this business.

Could a speaker break into the business on day one as a personality speaker?

They could position themselves as a personality speaker, but they're going to have to prove to the marketplace that they are qualified. Again, you can't be a pretender in this business and succeed. Audiences aren't stupid. You either have the skills or you don't, and if you're not trained when your opportunity presents itself, you're going down in flames. One speech has the power to catapult your career overnight. I know because it happened to me. If I wasn't trained, I would have bombed. Thank God I listened to Bill Gove. It literally changed my life.

Any other thoughts on personality vs. commodity speakers?

It's probably the most misunderstood concept in the business and maybe the most important. Study this idea and move closer toward it a little more every day.

SUMMARY

This is the most powerful concept I've heard Steve teach speakers, yet very few truly understand it. Of the speakers I've talked to over the past year, 80% claim they're personality speakers. They tell me how unique their message is and how no one can duplicate their delivery. They tell me how people rave about their speeches. Yet 99% of them are charging less than $5000 a speech. In fact, many are speaking for free or charging less than $500. I have no doubt these speakers are talented and I'm sure many of them have great messages. But I think they're misunderstanding what it means to be a personality speaker. It has less to do with the speaker's actual personality and more to do with their positioning. Personality speakers command high fees because organizations value their interpretations, ideas, and solutions.

Someone like Steve, for example, can charge $20,000 for a six-hour training. I hear speakers all the time say, "How can he charge so much when I can only get $2,000. There's no way the guy is $18,000 better than me." They're probably right and in some cases, may even be more talented than Steve. The difference between the $2,000 speaker/trainer and Steve is that the low-fee trainer is positioned as a commodity and Steve is positioned as a personality. People always ask, "How do I become a personality?" While there are many factors, the easiest and fastest way to do it would be to become a world-class keynote speaker. The moment Steve delivers a keynote speech at a national conference in front of the whole company and its executives, they'll want him to come back and train their people and no one else. This is the positioning we all want as opposed to the commodity speaker or trainer who is competing with every other speaker for the business, primarily on price.

If you're new to this business and haven't given many speeches, you're in a great place. The marketplace doesn't know you yet. The best advice I have for you is get professional training and learn how to become a personality speaker before you do anything else. This way, everything you're doing, you're doing the right way. More importantly, you're positioning yourself as a personality speaker right off the bat charging personality fees. This would seem like a logical first step, yet very few speakers do it. Most of the speakers I talked to over the past year who have already tried breaking into this business are going about it the wrong way. They're wasting time, money, and creating bad habits. But the most harmful part is they're positioning themselves in the marketplace as a commodity speaker. The sad part is that some of these people are extremely talented and have a great message to share, yet they will have a very hard time taking it to the next level if they get known as a commodity. Do yourself a favor and learn how to position yourself as a personality speaker from the start. It will be the fastest ways to catapult you to the next level.

SETTING UP THE BUSINESS

 One would think with the kind of money big speakers make that they have big businesses. Yet it seems like most speaker's businesses are "mom and pop" operations. Is this accurate?

 Absolutely. They are very profitable small businesses.

 How many employees do you have?

 There are four of us who work full-time on the business, and we have dozens of partners around the world.

 Why is this?

 I'm primarily a corporate market speaker, which requires fewer employees than a public market speaker holding large seminars.

Have you had employees in the past?

 At one point, we had 12 employees

 What happened?

 The additional profit wasn't paying for the additional overhead.

 Do most speakers have employees?

 No.

 How about hiring independent contractors to run their business?

 Most speakers run their own business.

In terms of positioning, it would seem as if a speaker who is less accessible would position himself or herself better. Is it important for a speaker to have someone who can screen calls and protect their time?

It depends on how many people you're reaching and how many calls you get every day. I answered the phone for the first three years of our business and it worked fine. Today we reach millions of people every year and receive thousands of phone calls. In the beginning, positioning shouldn't be a concern because you have nothing to position.

Is this something a speaker needs right off the bat or something they can do as they get bigger?

All a new speaker needs to do in the beginning is get professional platform training, build their speech and their speaking skills, and work on their content. Everything else is putting the cart before the horse.

I'd imagine you've had an office at one point?

Yes, we've had several offices.

Do you still have an office?

 We have an executive office service in Florida that answers our phone and receives our mail, but my wife and I work out of our Florida home in the winter and our Georgia home in the summer.

 Has having a home office hurt your positioning or do clients not care?

 They've never mentioned it. I'm not sure they know or care.

 With no employees or office, you must have some pretty low overhead.

 We have two full-time employees that work virtually out of their homes, but other than that our overhead is pretty low.

 What is your biggest expense?

 Income taxes.

Did any big speakers give you advice on how to set up and operate your business when you first started?

There's not much to setting up a speaking business. All you need is a cell phone and a laptop.

What was the best advice you ever received on setting up your speaking business?

The best advice was from Bill Gove, who told me to focus all my efforts in the beginning on learning the art of professional speaking and then rehearsing and practicing every day. After I got training and developed a 20-minute speech, he told me to speak at every chamber of commerce and civic club that would have me. I gave 200 free speeches over a 13-month period and learned the Bill Gove system. That was the most important thing I did to prepare myself for success. While many of the other new speakers in my NSA chapter were passing out business cards and attending speaker-marketing seminars, I was practicing. Most of them never made it in the business. Most new speakers focus on the sexy parts of the business, but the smart ones focus on the most important aspect: their speaking skills.

What's the biggest mistake you've made over the years with your business?

Taking bad advice for the first 12 months before Bill Gove set me on my path to success. Wasting my days trying to market myself when I was only a good amateur speaker not worthy of professional fees.

What are the first steps a speaker should take when they're setting up their business?

Get a cell phone, a laptop, and a quiet room in which to work. And get professional keynote speech training and start practicing every day.

What was the hardest part for you when you first started setting up your business?

Nothing. It took me a few hours, and that was before cell phones and laptops.

What's the most challenging part to running a speaking business?

In the beginning there isn't any business to run, so you spend all your time practicing, writing material, and giving free speeches. After you get busy, it's keeping up with your sales and marketing initiatives, promotional activities, and managing your money.

What does it cost to start a business?

Very little. Your biggest investment in the beginning should be training. Get the very best you can afford. After that, it's minimal unless you're marketing public seminars.

Does the business side take a lot of time? For example, invoicing, setting up flights, hotels, following up with people, etc.?

Not until you're busy, which is going to take some time. Starting a speaking business is not like starting a lawn-care company or carpet-cleaning service. It's a slow build because you have to establish yourself in a marketplace full of some of the smartest and most talented people in the world. You're not going to be discovered and no one is going to hand this to you. That's why you have to want it more than you've ever wanted anything in your life. You gotta wake up in the morning thinking about it and go to bed at night thinking about it. It has to become a 24/7 obsession, and you have to refuse to be denied. I live a millionaire's lifestyle today, but for the first ten years I was in this business, I don't know a speaker in the country that outworked me. I would never ask anyone to give this business what I've given it, but I will say that the harder you work at the things that matter, the faster you will grow. Your burning desire to succeed as a speaker is what you need more than anything else.

It seems like a lot of speakers' spouses help with these tasks.

If you can successfully work with your spouse, it can be a great advantage.

Speaking of spouses, what's your thought on including spouses in the speaking business?

Some couples can work together and some can't. Dawn (my wife) and I have been asked for years to conduct a seminar on how to work with your spouse in this business, but I don't think there's any secret outside of the basics of interpersonal communication. It's always been easy for us, but for other couples it's a disaster.

Do you think it's smart to have your spouse run your business?

As long as you get along and have the same work philosophy.

In talking to speakers over the years, does it seem like most spouses understand and support speakers as they're building their speaking business?

There's no empirical data on this, but many speakers I know struggle with their spouses and partners to educate them on how this business works.

What's the best advice you've heard on how speakers address spouses who don't get the business?

I would suggest they join NSA and meet some spouses of other speakers. They have spouse-only sessions at the national convention designed specifically to help non-speaker spouses understand the unique intricacies of this business from the spouse's perspective.

Anything else on setting up a speaking business?

Don't major in minors. Technology has made setting up a speaking business effortless. Once you start pulling in some decent income, you'll want to contact an attorney about setting up a sole proprietorship or LLC. You can do it even cheaper online. After that, get yourself a good accountant who understands the speaking business and have him do your books at least once a quarter to keep everything straight. I recommend Alan Feigenbaum in Florida. There are other good ones you can find through NSA. But remember that the heart of your success in this business will be your speaking skills. Without world-class speaking skills, all the set up and marketing is worthless.

SUMMARY

Few speakers I talk to focus on developing world-class speaking skills. The majority are concerned with marketing and learning the logistics of setting up a speaking business. I included this chapter because I knew Steve would downplay the importance of the logistics and bring the focus back to developing platform skills and a world-class keynote. Don't be fooled by anyone who says your focus should be on anything else other than your speech and delivery at the start. They're just trying to sell you something. If that's where you're putting your focus, know that you're wasting your money and creating unnecessary overhead while a select group of speakers are developing their skills. The group working on their skills will be moving forward while the majority of people working on their business will have a great marketing plan with nothing to market.

It seems as if I've heard every question and concern speakers have about starting their speaking business. The one that seems most challenging for speakers is the challenge speakers in relationships have with getting their significant other on board. I can't tell you how many times over the past year I've talked to speakers who had the burning desire and were ready to pursue their dream as a speaker. Five months later, they were in the same place. People opened up to me and shared that they still had the dream and wanted to start so badly, but their significant other was not 100% onboard or supporting them to spend time and money to pursue their dream.

I don't blame them. There is so much misinformation in this business. If the majority of speakers in our industry don't understand it, how can we expect our significant others and those outside the industry to? Many of our significant others have seen us speak and get standing ovations. They tell us we're better than most fee paid speakers they've seen and we love them for it. The problem is they never learn how this business works and how complex it really is. They have the best intentions but never really give us their full support allowing us to spend time and money doing what we need to do because from the outside, it looks so easy.

Here are two things I've found helpful for getting my wife onboard. I would recommend them to anyone who is in a relationship and pursing their speaking dream.

Number one: Educate them on the business and the lifestyle of a speaker. The first thing I would do is have them read Steve's story at the beginning of this book. Let them see what this business is really like. Let them know the reality of how tough this business is but also how rewarding and awesome the lifestyle can be. I can't think of a better lifestyle than that of a top speaker. You can travel the world with your significant other, commanding high fees and spreading your message to thousands of people, speaking in some of the most prestigious halls and stadiums.

Number two: Show them your step-by-step plan. The challenge I believe most speakers have is that they wake up in the morning and have no idea what they need to do that day to move forward. If they have a plan but came up with it on their own, they're still shooting in the dark hoping they land in the right place. Spouses can sense this. They can sense the uncertainty. While I have intentionally not charged any fees for my speaking yet, my wife is extremely supportive. I think part of this is because I am a graduate of the Bill Gove Speech Workshop and she knows I am following a proven step-by-step system that has produced some of the most well-known and highest-grossing speakers of all time. Every day when I wake up, I know exactly what I need to be doing in order to move closer to becoming a personality keynote speaker. While there have been times of tension with no money rolling in, I have 100% of her support since she knows I'm on the road to success in this business.

To recap, educate your significant other on the business and show them you're not just wasting time but are actually following a proven system that will get you closer to becoming the next top speaker.

BUILDING A FAN BASE

What is a fan base?

It's a group of people who follow your speaking, writing and recording career

Is it different than a database?

A database is a collection of emails, addresses, phone numbers, or other method of contact data. You can purchase a database, but you have to grow a fan base.

How important is it for a speaker to have a fan base?

It's critical if you're working in the public market, especially if you want to sell books, recordings, or seminars

How many people does a speaker need in their fan base to be a big speaker?

It's not just about numbers, but about the connection you have to your fan base. That being said, 10,000 fans who follow your career and believe in your point of view is a good start. The speakers with the strongest point of view usually have the most loyal fan bases and sell the most books and recording.s

How many people does the average speaker have in their fan base?

Less than 500.

Why don't most speakers have large fan bases?

They have trouble building fan bases because they are writing and saying the same things as other speakers. We refer to them as "commodity speakers," which means they are relegated to low fees and low sales.

Is it easier to build a fan base in the public or corporate market?

The corporate market primarily hires one way: through referrals. The public market is where you want to build your fan base to sell seminar seats, books and recordings

Does this mean corporate speakers have smaller fan bases or do they market to the public market as well?

Most corporate speakers only work in that market. Very few speakers work in both the public and corporate market.

Should you have a certain number of people in your fan base before you start creating products?

At least 3,000-5,000 people who are solid fans who you have data on to be able to contact. Otherwise you're going to have a garage full of books, CD's and videos.

Why?

The average speaker sells 250 copies of their book and very few CD's or DVDs. Writing a book just for marketing purposes is overrated. Writing a good book is a difficult, arduous process that requires discipline and dedication.

Why not sell it around the world and make a million in the process? You need a fan base to do that.

When you first broke into the business, you had one of the largest databases of any speaker. How did you build this?

I bought some of it from a list company and the rest I swapped with other speakers.

Was it a good strategy? Was it an engaged database?

No. I had a database of 212,000 people who didn't know who I was and didn't care.

Is it more important to have a large database or an engaged database?

You want a large database of engaged fans who believe in your point of view.

What percent of your database is really engaged?

Probably a pretty high percentage because I have a really strong point of view. There are people who love me and people that hate me. The people that love me are on my database

How does a speaker build a fan base?

One speech, seminar, TV, radio, or print interview at a time. It takes years to develop a loyal fan base.

What's one of the best strategies for a speaker to build a fan base online?

A unique point of view that challenges conventional wisdom is the cornerstone of building a loyal fan base. Without that, all the marketing techniques and strategies are meaningless. After you've developed a strong point of view, a video blog on your topic is hard to beat. Your fans get to see and hear you. It's like having your own TV station that broadcasts anytime you wish.

Do you give away free information to build your fan base?

 We do, and it works well. It's only one strategy, but it gives people that don't know you a chance to test-drive you and your material. If they like it, they usually buy something or attend a seminar.

 You have several different blogs? Has this been a good tool for building a fan base?

 Incredible. Video blogs are powerful tools for speakers and very few people use them. Who has the time or patience to read a blog? Video is the future!

 You use to do a podcast, and now you do a video blog. Do you get a more involved fan base with the videos?

 Yes. Your fans get to hear and see you. I take my little blog video camera with me everywhere. Every time I give a speech, people come out of the audience and say; "I subscribe to your video blog, and I've followed you all over the world. I feel like I know you!"

How did speakers in the past build databases before they had the internet?

We used direct mail, which is expensive and risky. I used to send 30,000 sales letters out every month and pray we would at least break even. Some months we made big money and other months we got killed. I lost a lot of sleep in those days!

Have you built the majority of your fan base from people seeing your speeches, reading your books, and finding you online, or is it a combination of all three?

It's a combination. There's no easy answer. You just gotta keep showing up and bringing value.

Do you use paid online advertising to market your services and build your database? Is it necessary and worth paying to build your fan base?

Yes, for some of our programs. We advertise to get them to experience a free program. If they like it, they usually become fans and subscribe to one or more of our email newsletters or blogs.

What's your best advice on building a database?

Give people a reason to subscribe to your email list, video blog, or radio show. What are you offering that's unique and exciting? The competition for people's attention is high, so you have to differentiate yourself in this industry to gain attention in the marketplace.

Can an aspiring keynote speaker start building a database before they are actually delivering keynotes?

Theoretically, yes, but developing the keynote should be your first priority.

How important is social media when developing a database?

It's very powerful.

Do you have to have a strong point of view before you build a database?

I would recommend it, because if you're simply repeating what every other speaker is saying, your message is going to get lost.

Do you have different databases for different parts of your business?

 Yes. We have segmented into three parts based on how we collect the data.

 Do you have different databases for different markets?

 Yes.

 How often should you contact your database?

 There's a lot of debate about this and I certainly don't have the definitive answer. However, I would suggest that the more sophisticated your database, the less often I would recommend contacting them. For example, our database is among the most sophisticated in the industry. It's full of doctors, lawyers, college professors, corporate executives, entrepreneurs, and millionaires. Read the comments on Mental Toughness Blog.com and you'll get an idea of how educated and successful our fan base is. With that in mind, we only post blog videos and send emails once a week. These are busy people who don't want to be pestered. Once a week works for us. Speakers with less sophisticated databases send emails out every day and it works for them. You just have to know the level of your audience.

What's the worst advice you've heard on building a database?

Giving away something cheesy or unrelated to your expertise. The bait you fish with determines the catch. If you want to draw successful people, don't insult them with get rich quick schemes or doomsday scenarios. Hyperbole and easy money schemes work with uneducated, naïve people, and if that's who you want to attract, go for it. But remember that 99% of these people are broke and can't afford to attend your seminars or buy your products. I suggest that you go after the best and brightest and see if you're smart enough to gain and hold their attention. These are society's winners, and if you can capture them, you've done something special. Why not play in the big leagues and see how good you are? Anyone can cater to society's lowest common denominator. Televangelists have been doing it for years.

Are there people who build lists in an unethical way?

Yeah, there are spammers, but they don't last long in this business. There's a group of Internet marketers posing as speakers that use questionable tactics to get people on their list, but the recession has wiped most of them out because they were selling garbage.

How are speakers different than Internet marketers who build big databases?

 It all comes down to your offering in the marketplace. There are Internet marketers and speakers who offer quality information and others who don't. The main difference is usually in the level of sophistication. A speaker who speaks to Fortune 500 companies is probably going to offer the highest level products and information because corporate executives who hire them will reject anything less. A public market speaker and Internet marketer can sell get-rich-quick information all day long and get away with it. So in that sense, they are no different, yet I'd like to think professional speakers hold themselves to a higher standard than most Internet marketers

 What does your database typically want from you? Do they want your content? Your point on controversial issues? Your help?

 It depends on what they have come to expect from you. My fan base loves mental toughness and critical thinking, and they expect me to always be pushing back and challenging conventional wisdom. I don't ask them to believe anything I say; I only ask them to consider it and think for themselves. If they disagree, I want them to challenge me, and if you read the Mental Toughness blog, you will see that they do. I'm not looking for hero-worship, and they're not looking for a hero. I'm a thought leader on a subject they're interested in, and I offer my ideas and opinions in multiple mediums for their consideration. They read my books, listen to my speeches, and watch my TV interviews and video blogs, and then they offer their own opinions, and we debate the issue until we've hit it from every possible angle. It's a healthy and respectful discourse.

You've commented on controversial issues that have upset and offended certain people on your database. It doesn't seem like you're concerned about keeping your fan base happy. Is this true?

My role as a thought leader on mental toughness and critical thinking isn't to make people happy. My job is to openly challenge the status quo for the purpose of helping my fan base get better results in their lives. This approach offends some people because they lack the emotional maturity and intelligence to consider an opposing point of view without becoming overly emotional. Most people have a set of beliefs that help them make sense of the world, and this makes them comfortable. When someone like me comes along and challenges those beliefs, it scares them because if what I'm saying is correct, their world no longer makes sense, and that terrifies the emotionally immature. That's why when I do a controversial video blog, some people will viciously attack me and threaten to burn my books and tell all their friends not to buy anything else from me. They want to punish me for scaring them with new ideas and for suggesting that their view of an issue may be wrong. It's the mindset of a child, and I'm glad when they leave our list. What they are looking for is a motivational speaker that delivers high school-level positive thinking platitudes they can scotch tape on their refrigerator, and that's not me. I refuse to pander to these people or anyone on my video blog, and that's why we attract some of the smartest people in the public and corporate market. Smart people welcome opposition and love intelligent, respectful discourse, and I love being the speaker who facilitates it. The easily offended and faint of heart need not apply.

Do you need everyone?

Oh, God. No. There are seven billion people in the world. If you have 50,000 people a month following your speeches, TV interviews, books, audios and video blog, and other delivery mechanisms, you are set for life. If you have a strong point of view and are delivering it unapologetically, you will never get them all. The good news is, you don't need them all. All you need is a 50,000 people a month, and you're a millionaire.

Do you have a responsibility to your database?

I think so. I can't speak for anyone else, but my responsibility is to always tell them the truth, as least as I see it, and always be pushing the boundaries of limited thinking, age-old dogma, and fear-based beliefs.

How do you build credibility with your database?

By always over-delivering in everything you do. Always give them ten times what they pay for and they will reward you with their loyalty.

Any other thoughts on building a database?

In the post economic crash world of this industry, only the true thought leaders will thrive. Decide what makes you different and have the guts to stick to it no matter how much criticism you receive from people who disagree with your interpretation. All the positive thinking platitudes have been said, and as great as they are, every high school senior knows them by heart. We're no longer living in the information age, we are now living in the instant-information age, where a 10-year-old kid can find the answer to any question he has in 30 seconds on his smart phone. Building a big fan base is not about tactics and strategies; it's about offering a unique perspective on your subject matter that people find valuable. Don't attempt to trick your fans or play games with them. Say what you mean, say it hot, and let them decide for themselves. If you'll do this, I'll see you at the Million Dollar Speakers' Group, and I'll be the first one to welcome you to the club. We need more smart people to take a stand and lead the conversation. The speaking business is undergoing a metamorphosis, and we need more great minds to help us lead the way.

SUMMARY

Fan base! Fan base! Fan base! This is the new currency in business. If you have no fans, you have no one to sell to. Always be thinking of ways you can build your fan base. If you're speaking, even at a free event, make sure you have a way for people who want more to give you their contact information. I've heard so many speakers tell me they've spoken hundreds of times and how everyone in the audience raves about their speech. I ask how many people they have in their database and they say zero! If you give a speech and dazzle the audience, yet don't have people signing up for your services or mailings, you're probably a great speaker but you're not differentiating your message enough from the masses. When your audience hears your unique interpretation and thinks to themselves, "I've never heard anyone else describe it this way," you're setting yourself up as a one of a kind. It's easy to create a fan base because your fans have nowhere else to go. No one else is going to be able to help them solve their problem the same way you can.

Speakers are sold by marketers and vendors on how important it is to have products. I've seen so many speakers lose thousands of dollars creating products and then realizing they have one big problem: no one to sell them to! The first thing you need to do is create a fan base of at least 1,000 people. Then when you have a following, you can create a product and actually have people to sell to.

Don't be delusional and fall into the trap that most speakers do of believing you have a following when you really don't. Your friends and family are great and will hopefully support you through the growth of your business. But ask yourself, how many fans do I actually have following me outside of my family and friends? I've heard from too many speakers who say everyone loves their message and wants them to write a book or create a product. Fantastic! Obviously you're onto something big. I'd just make sure I have someone to sell them to.

SETTING FEES

 How much did you charge for your first speech?

 $10 per person.

 Why $10?

 That's all I could get.

 How many people attended your first speech?

 Six.

So your first paid speech made you $60.

No, because I had to pay for the room. I think it was $30.

Were you disappointed?

Are you kidding? I was thrilled! Earning $30 to talk to people about a subject I'd studied for years was one of the coolest things I had ever done!

What was your first paid corporate speech?

It was for Volvo dealership. They paid me $250.

That must have been exciting.

I was pumped up for a week!

And how did your fees progress from there?

 I started charging $250 for a keynote and $500 for a day. Plus, I was selling my Siebold System for Mental Toughness for $250 in the back of the room. At the time, I thought my fees were pretty high.

 What did you dream of charging?

 $5,000

 Did you think you'd just keep increasing your fees till you got there?

 Yes.

 How did that work for you?

 It didn't work at all. And it never would have. I just didn't know it at the time.

What happened? How did you go from charging $250 to $5000 a speech?

I met Bill Gove, went to his workshop and learned how to write and deliver a world-class keynote speech.

So you jumped right to $5000?

No, Bill suggested I pull myself out of the business until I was good enough to charge $5,000.

Is this how most speakers do it?

No. But most speakers fail.

Is it realistic for a speaker to go from charging nothing to $5,000?

No, it takes time and practice. You have to actually be worth $5,000. How many people earn $5,000 an hour for what they do for a living? Very few. If you're not worth it, they won't pay it.

Most speakers I know want to be able to increase their fees significantly overnight. Can you do this or does it take time for the marketplace to get to know you as a personality speaker?

 Nothing in this business happens overnight. It takes time to command significant fees.

 It seems as if most aspiring speakers get excited if someone offers them $750 to deliver a speech. Are you suggesting it's bad for them to accept these fees? Will it position them in the marketplace as a $750 speaker?

 If they are willing to settle for low fees, they should take it. If they aspire to earn big money in this business, they should decline and re-enter the business when they're worth $5,000.

 Many speakers request information from clients before revealing their fee. For example, they ask how many people will be attending and what the client's budget is. Why do they do this and do you agree with this strategy?

 Many low fee speakers follow this philosophy. If you want to play in the big leagues, this is a terrible strategy. You don't walk into a Porsche dealership and negotiate, but the local Ford dealership will haggle with you all day long. If you want to sell to the richest and most sophisticated buyers, publish your fee and play it straight. Anything else is an insult to the buyer.

Do you negotiate your fees?

Does Nordstrom's?

Why not?

Because it's terrible positioning. That's why Nordstrom's doesn't do it.

So you charge the same fee for all your clients?

Of course. And Nordstrom's charges the same price for all customers.

Do you make exceptions for certain groups like non-profits?

Yes, for charities.

Many speakers speak for free if they're in front of a large enough audience. Is this a good idea? Can this be profitable for speakers if they sell their products in the back of the room?

That's a different opportunity. Most speakers who address large groups speak for free. If the audience is large enough, it's not a bad idea.

What are the entry level fees for personality speakers?

$5,000-$7,500

Is it different for the public and corporate market?

Absolutely. Corporate fees are much higher. Most public market speakers don't charge a fee. They make their money on back-of-room sales.

Do corporations overlook speakers who are charging less?

They consider low-fee speakers a risk.

How do you know when you're ready to start charging personality fees?

 When someone who knows tells you.

 How do you know if you're worth $5,000?

 You need to consult someone who knows what you're worth in the marketplace.

 I've had marketers tell me I could be easily charging $8,000 a speech. How do I know if this is good advice?

 You need to consult an expert who knows. How many people do you know who charge $8,000 an hour for what they do? It's pretty rare.

 Whom should I be listening to?

 An expert in this business.

How does a speaker get in front of this type of person?

 By paying them.

 I often hear speakers say, "I'm equally talented as that speaker charging $7,500." Can speakers base their fees off of other speakers?

 Talent is overrated. This business is about skill, and if you're new, I promise you you're not as skilled as a high-paid presenter. Be careful not to delude yourself. This is a real business with real buyers. If you're new, don't kid yourself into believing you're as good as a seasoned presenter. Just because you won a ribbon at Toastmasters doesn't mean anyone will pay to speak.

 Are there are certain expectations from the buyer if you're charging more than $5000?

 The more you charge the more they expect.

You're currently charging $15,000 for a keynote speech. How will you know when it's time to increase your fee?

When demand exceeds supply.

Is this the same system you'd advise other speakers to use when they're increasing their fees?

Yes.

With the way the economy is, are you adjusting your fees to get more business?

We don't adjust fees, but the business is more difficult to get since the crash.

What about other million-dollar speakers?

The ones I've talked to say the same thing. We're doing well, but we're working harder for the same money.

Historically, are fees increasing or decreasing for speakers?

 Fees have been dropping or stagnant since the crash.

 So you're saying some of the biggest speakers of the past, like Bill Gove, didn't have the opportunity to make as much as speakers today?

 No, they didn't. The big non-celebrity speakers of the past made a good living. The top non-celebrity speakers of today are multimillionaires.

 The average person can't comprehend a speaker making five, ten, fifteen thousand dollars a speech. How can speakers charge so much? Are they really worth it?

 Yes. It's supply and demand, like any other product or service.

 Any other advice for speakers as they're setting up their fees?

 Seek out the advice of someone who knows the business before you set your fees. Their advice is worth its weight in gold.

SUMMARY

It seems to me like the average speaker trying to break into the business has no idea how to set their fees. They think about it in a very linear way. They start out speaking for free, and then some organization offers them $750 to speak. They're all pumped up and excited to be getting paid $750 for a 40-minute speech. This is great if you're okay with being a commodity speaker and charging smaller fees. But if you're looking to be a personality speaker charging substantial fees, then this is one of the worst things you can do. The marketplace now knows them as a $750 speaker. They've now joined the group of speakers in this business that spends years trying to figure out how to increase their fees. They're now on the linear path of gradually increasing their fees from $750 to $1000, to $2000, all the way up to $5000.

I think the key to being able to charge high fees is to break in on day one at $5000. This obviously isn't easy to do. To get to this point, Bill Gove made Steve do 200 free speeches. But once he did this, he started charging $5000 a speech and has gone up ever since. While the average speaker has no patience to speak for free and starts down the linear path of slowly increasing their fees, Steve was becoming a world-class speaker and catapulted from $0 to $5000 in 13 months.

Be careful to whom you listen when it comes to setting your fees. I just talked to a speaker who had recently attended a seminar where the leader told the speaker they were shocked they weren't making over a million dollars speaking. The speaker was telling me this over the phone as a way to demonstrate to me how good he was. After I got off the phone, I went online and discovered it was a seminar put on by an internet marketer selling social media information to speakers. Of course this seminar leader would tell the speaker this! The more the speaker buys into the idea that he should be making a million dollars and is not doing so because of his social media campaign, the more the speaker will buy. The only person you should be listening to are the people that do this for a living or people that hire speakers. If you're looking to speak to a Fortune 500 sales team, most likely a VP of Sales is going to hire you. That would be a good person to ask. If you can't get connected to the type of buyer in your industry, go to someone like Steve who is at the top of this business charging high fees and he'll be able to give you a pretty good idea of where you're at.

The last point I want to make is, don't think you can fool people with your fee. The moment you're up on stage and it's just you and an audience, you better be able to meet the expectations of the fee you're charging. There is no fooling the audience. I've talked to several people who think they're just going to start charging $5000 because they know how to market themselves the right way. All I have to say is, good luck. You may fool someone into hiring you once, but you won't be able to do it twice.

MARKETING

How do most speakers market themselves?

In all the wrong ways. Websites, demo videos, and through services that claim to match them with people who can hire them.

Is this effective?

No, it's a complete waste of time and money.

If it doesn't work, then why do speakers market themselves this way?

Because they don't know any better. They are listening to the wrong people who profit from get-rich-quick misinformation.

Do speakers get discovered?

No. No more than any other vendor gets discovered. Does a plumber get discovered?

How realistic is it that a top speaker will discover a speaker and want to help them?

Top speakers aren't looking for protégés, they are looking for business.

How about an executive. Will they discover a speaker from going online and finding their website or discovering them on a site with a list of speakers?

Absolutely not. I've been interviewing executives from some of the biggest companies in the world for the last 12 years, and they all say the same thing: they only hire speakers that are referred from a trusted colleague. That's why we started SSN in 2011. Now we have over 300 members that serve as referral agents for speakers who want to break into new companies but don't know anyone on the inside.

Do you market yourself on websites that list speakers for executives and organizations to find?

No. It's a waste of time. Executives don't search websites. They run multimillion-dollar divisions of companies.

Why do so many speakers buy into this and list themselves on sites that claim to have organizations and executives looking for speakers?

Because they don't know any better.

How are million-dollar speakers marketing themselves differently than the masses who are failing in the business?

Top speakers get business by referral. I haven't done a paid speaking date without a referral since 1997.

Is this how they get engagements?

Yes.

How important are referrals?

They are the backbone of the industry.

How did you break into major corporations?

My first major national convention keynote was for Toyota. Larry Wilson referred me to the president of the company.

Can you reach an executive at a major corporation without a referral?

You have a better chance of winning the lottery. But even if you reach them, it's unlikely he or she will take you seriously without a referral.

Can you cold-call?

Not to senior executives. Even if you were skilled enough to reach them, you wouldn't have any credibility if you did it through a cold call.

What is a paid referral?

 There are only two types of referrals: paid and unpaid. If your phone is ringing off the hook with organic referrals, you're all set. If not, paid referrals is the way to go. You simply sign a contract with a referral agent who gets you in the door and pay him or her a percentage of your profits.

 Do they work?

 I've made millions from paid referrals and so have others.

 Do most speakers use paid referrals?

 Just the smart ones!

 Who would you give referrals to?

 A credible expert in a non-competitive topic.

Would you ever refer a speaker who is just trying to break in?

I've referred dozens of speakers, some of them new and some experienced. It would depend if he or she were competent.

You started the Siebold Success Network. (SSN) What is it?

It's a paid referral network for speakers, trainers, coaches, and consultants

Does it work?

Very well. We've done around $2.8 million dollars in referral business between speakers.

Have speakers caught on to this idea or has there been resistance?

300 speakers have caught on and thousands have resisted. Paid referrals are the future of this business, but most speakers don't know it yet. This is another reason so many speakers have gone broke or out of business since the great recession.

How is it different than a speaker's bureau?

Speakers bureaus are non-exclusive speaker's agencies who deal with a tiny group of speakers. SSN is a paid referral network than any speaker can utilize.

Speaking of speakers' bureaus, what are your thoughts on them?

I think they're great for the select group of speakers they serve.

Do bureaus typically take on new speakers to represent?

No. Speakers' bureaus are like banks. They only want you when you don't need them.

What are most bureaus looking for from speakers?

They are looking for speakers who are already successful and willing to partner with them and turn over their leads to the bureau. It's a good model for a small group of speakers.

Almost every aspiring speaker I talk to says they're focusing on their website. Is this the first thing they should be focusing on?

 Absolutely not. Speakers are their own product, and if the product isn't world-class, the website and other marketing strategies will only make them fail faster. What new speakers need is training. Most of them have no idea how good they have to be to break into this business as a professional. That's why 99% of them never make it.

 It seems like the next thing they focus on is getting a demo video? How important is this?

 Again, this is a waste of time and money until they are good enough to charge fees. They need to learn how to deliver a professional speech before they start marketing themselves.

 Can a demo video make or break you?

 It can hurt you if it's not well done. It's not going to make your career no matter how good it is. A lot of money is wasted on demo videos.

Many speakers write books and send them to prospects with a one sheet and a demo video. Is this an effective strategy?

This identifies you as an amateur. Never send a book or anything unsolicited to an executive. It's a terrible marketing strategy used by speakers who don't know better. You're not cleaning carpets; you're selling a world-class specialty service. Your marketing needs to reflect that.

How do you know who to listen to when it comes to marketing?

Listen to successful speakers who have penetrated the markets you want to break into. Most people teaching speakers how to market have never done it themselves. You can blow a lot of money listening to the wrong people.

Do you market yourself differently now compared to when you first got started in the business?

Yes. In the beginning I chased down every lead I could find. Today I only accept the speaking dates I really want.

In reality, is the marketing or speaking more important to becoming a million- dollar speaker?

 The speaking is the product, and if you're not a highly trained professional, your marketing means nothing. Speakers who attempt to break into this business without professional training rarely make it.

 Should speakers focus on the speaking or marketing first?

 Your speaking skills will make or break you. First, you build the product and then you market it.

 Has it gotten easier or tougher to market yourself with new technology?

 Easier in the public market. The corporate market is still driven by referral.

 What's the biggest mistake speakers make with their marketing?

 They market themselves before they're good enough on the platform.

Do you generate a lot of business from going to speaker networking events?

 Not unless you're doing paid referrals.

 How much should a speaker expect to spend on marketing?

 Not much in the corporate market. Your main expense should be referral fees.

 I hear a lot of speakers say they need to brand themselves. Is branding important?

 You want your clients and fans to connect to you and your topic. Branding is for big companies that want to burn their products into the collective consciousness of the market they serve. It has nothing to do with our business, but people selling branding to speakers who don't know any better have made millions.

I've heard speakers hiring an image consultant at the start of their career? Have you hired one?

 No, and I don't know any major speaker who has. Successful speakers invest their money in areas that matter, such as training.

 Any other advice for speakers when it comes to marketing?

 In the speaking business, you are the product, therefore your ability to deliver your philosophy and expertise is the most important thing. Build a great product (you) and your marketing efforts will catapult your results. But if you are a mediocre speaker with the same message as everyone else, all your marketing will tell people is you're a low-fee commodity speaker. Invest your time and money in your own development, and you have a real shot at succeeding.

SUMMARY

If you want to make a million-dollars selling to speakers, sell them marketing advice. This is the one, and unfortunately, only thing every aspiring speaker I talk to seems to think they need help with. I've talked to speakers who have been in this business for years yet are still making no money. When I ask what the problem is and what they need help with, they almost always answer with one of two things. They say, "I just need to learn how to market myself" or "I just need to figure out how to get in the door and get hired."

The biggest myth I've seen speakers fall victim to is the idea that they're going to get discovered. I grilled Steve on this question because I hear it from so many people. Speakers spend all this money on demo videos, websites, and being listed on speaker websites and then sit idly by waiting for someone to discover them. If you're one of these speakers, how's this working for you? I'm guessing it's probably not working very well. A speaker is hired from an executive going to someone whom he or she trusts, who is under a similar amount of pressure, and is asking for a referral. This is how speakers are hired at the highest level. They are hired from referrals.

This is what speakers should be focusing on when they're concerned about marketing: creating a paid referral network. If you're getting flooded with organic referrals, you're in good shape. If not, take control of your business and start doing paid referrals. Build up a paid referral network so that you always have people looking for referrals and business for you. Don't just rely on four or five people. Create an army. Build it yourself, or go to www.ssnlive.org and learn how you can get connected to referral agents all around the world.

If this sounds like an easy concept, it is. But don't be fooled into thinking it's as easy as doing deals with referral agents and your phone is going to be ringing off the hook. For some people, it will. When Steve started doing paid referrals back in 2001, he had to stop taking leads from referral agents because he was getting too many leads and was having trouble servicing them all. The key to his success, and the other speakers who do this, is that they are world-class speakers. If you were willing to give me 20% of your speaking fee for a lead, I'd think that was a great deal. But I'd be crazy to open my rolodex and give you a lead if I didn't feel confident in your ability to deliver a world-class speech.

My suggestion to you is focus on becoming a world-class speaker. Once you're at this level, focus on referrals.

LICENSING

You are one of the few speakers I know who has made seven figures as both a licensee and licensor. Tell me, what was the first product you licensed?

The Bill Gove Speech Workshop.

Why did you license it?

It had a 55-year track record of world-class success, and it had created more million-dollar speakers than any program in history. This was the keynote speaking system that launched my career, and I believed I could make it more successful than ever.

Did you know when you purchased it that you'd make your money back and be successful with it?

I hoped so.

Were you looking to license something or was this an unexpected opportunity?

Not really. When Bill Gove died in 2001, I had promised him I would keep the workshop going.

Did you consider licensing any other material or programs when you first started speaking?

Of course. Licensing a successful speaker's intellectual property is one of the smartest things you can do. It can save you years of writing, creating, and testing your own content.

Tell us more about that. Why didn't you purchase them?

The Bill Gove Speech Workshop was a perfect fit. The others were not.

Is it important that the material or program fit your style as a speaker?

 It's critical.

 Looking back, how has licensing the Bill Gove Speech Workshop impacted your business?

 It's a small percentage of our business, but it's earned millions of dollars for our company. It's been a very good investment.

 I'm guessing you have no regrets about it?

 Oh, no. I love the workshop. It is far and away the best keynote speaking workshop in the business. Nothing is even close. Bill Gove was the best of the best. He was the father of the industry and the genius of the keynote speech. That's why people call the Bill Gove Speech Workshop, "the Harvard of Professional Speaking Schools."

Now you also have been extremely successful as a licensor. What is it that people license from you?

The Mental Toughness University and College Programs, The Fat Loser Coaching Program, and the Bill Gove Speech Workshop.

How did you come up with this?

People started asking me if I would consider licensing our programs about ten years ago, and we have had multiple offers to buy our company. Instead of selling the company, we started licensing a select group of people.

Are other speakers doing this?

Very few.

Why so few?

You have to have a serious record of success to license intellectual property, and most speakers are barely eking out a living. Others don't have a large enough database to market their license program to.

This is a personality-driven business. Wouldn't licensing your material only promote you and your material as opposed to the speaker who licensed it?

 It depends on how it's promoted. We partner with our licensees and teach them how to use our content to promote their business. One of our new licensees made over $212,000 last year part-time.

 How would licensing your material, for example, benefit a speaker?

 The minute you become a licensee, you become our partner, which means you are in business with one of the highest-grossing non-celebrity speakers in the world. You become part of the family. This allows you to leverage our credibility, client list, and content. If the content fits your passion, it's one of the best investments you can make in this business.

 What is the downside of a speaker licensing your material?

 There is no downside unless you don't do the work.

How much should someone expect to pay for a license?

It varies depending on the program. You can pay anywhere from $25,000 to well over $250,000.

It seems to me like the power in a license is in the details of the contract. What should speakers look for and be careful of in a contract?

You want the license to offer you maximum flexibility to give you the best chance for success. You need to feel good about the speaker who is selling you the license and have a sense of trust in what you're buying and whom you're buying it from.

Any other thoughts on licensing?

There are fortunes to be earned in licensing content. I'm planning on purchasing several other licenses in the future and I would recommend it to everyone.

SUMMARY

This business is all about credibility. If you're just starting and looking for credibility, consider licensing proven material so you have someplace to start. I still believe your first priority should be to develop your speaking skills. But once you are ready for the big stage, having a proven program, especially to sell on the back end, can be worth its weight in gold. If you decide to go this route, make sure you do it the right way. I've talked to several speakers who tell me they are a licensee of speaker XYZ or a licensee of their program. This is a big mistake. They think by mentioning the name of the person from whom they licensed their program, they're making themselves more credible. This is a personality-based business and all they are doing by mentioning the person they licensed their material from is building up that speaker's business, not their own. Make sure you have the flexibility to insert the content or program into your own program. That way you are building up your own program and personality and not someone else.

As a licensee of Steve's mental toughness material, here are my three suggestions if you're thinking about licensing material:

One: Make sure what your licensing has a proven track record. The biggest advantage of licensing material is creating a client list overnight. You want to purchase a proven system and without an impressive client list and track record of success, it will be hard for you to leverage.

Two: The terms are everything. Make sure you understand the terms so you know what you can and can't do. Make sure you have the power to do what you want to do. Also, make sure you understand the money. You need to know if there are any territories, royalties, renewal fees, etc.

Three: Make sure the material you're licensing is a good fit for you. Licensing Steve's Mental Toughness material was a no-brainer for me since it fits perfectly with my style and interest. Had it not, there is no way I would have licensed it.

Four: If you leverage it the right way, this is one of the smartest strategies for catapulting yourself to the next level.

I would strongly consider licensing proven material, if you haven't already. This is one of the smartest ways to leverage someone else's time and work. What may have taken someone twenty years to produce, you can own overnight. If you license the right content or program, it can be worth a fortune.

MEDIA

 Of all the speakers out there, you are probably the most qualified to talk to about the media. You are in the media more than any other speaker I know. How many interviews do you do every year?

 About 500.

 Why do you do it?

 Several reasons. To get my message to the masses, to build credibility with corporate clients, to expand my fan base, and to help stimulate conversation on some of the most important issues facing society.

Do you generate business from it?

 Yes, we have generated millions of dollars in new business from publicity.

 Can you give me an example of how you monetize the media?

 Sure. A corporate executive calls because he's considering me for his national convention keynote. He's never seen me speak, but another executive referred me.

I say, "Are you in front of your computer?"

He says, "Yes."

"Type in www.steveontv.com."

The first thing out of his mouth is "Wow!" My credibility with this executive is catapulted within seconds, and that's usually all it takes to close the deal. The media exposure doesn't sell the speech, but it helps the executive emotionally justify his or her decision.

 Are a lot of speakers doing this?

 No.

Why not?

They think it's about selling books, and when they try it and don't sell many, they see it as a waste of time and money.

Why is media so important for a speaker?

The ability to charge world-class fees is based on credibility, and an interview on Fox Business Network or in The Wall Street Journal or Fortune Magazine is an implied endorsement from that major media outlet.

Is there a specific type of media you target, for example, TV, radio, magazines, newspapers, etc.?

TV, magazines, and newspapers.

Do you use a publicist?

Yes.

Is this important?

It is if you're building a serious speaking career. If all you want is some local press, you can do it yourself.

Are there specific publicists for speakers?

Yes, there are publicists who specialize in promoting authors and speakers.

Your publicist has received some of the top awards for your media campaigns. Is that what it is to you, a media campaign?

Yes.

Do you have a strategy?

Yes.

Your publicist recently presented a case study of your media campaign to the National Speakers Association Million Dollar Speaker Group. How did that go?

The case study showed an 1100% return on our investment. Speakers like Brian Tracy and Harvey Mackay were extremely impressed, and if you can impress them, it's a pretty good presentation.

Tell me about it. How much had you spent on media in the case study?

We invested around $100,000 and earned approximately $1.2 million directly from people saying we hired you or purchased as a result of seeing you in the press.

Could you track how much business that media exposure generated for you?

Like advertising, it's impossible to track all of the business generated, but we ask as many customers as possible what led them to us.

Were other speakers impressed? Is this something most of them were already doing?

Yes, they were blown away. The Million Dollar Speakers' Group is a closed meeting made up of speakers earning at least one million dollars per year with the tax returns to prove it. We're talking about 39 of the smartest, savviest, sophisticated speakers in the world, and they understood it. Most of them use publicity at some level.

 Did you ever try getting in the media on your own?

 Yes.

 How did that work?

 Not bad, but I only did it on a local scale. To mount a national campaign, it requires the skills of a pro.

 Can you do it on your own?

 It's possible, but you have to ask yourself what you want to do for a living: speak or chase publicity? And like professional speaking, it's harder than it appears.

How much should a speaker expect to pay for a good publicist?

 It varies, but 5K to 10K a month is not uncommon.

 Do you recommend someone have a publicist year round or hire them when their topic is hot in the media?

 You have to be ready before you hire publicist or you're wasting your time and money. The first step is keynote speech training, so you know what you're doing. If you're not competent as a keynoter, you will bomb when you get your break. Most people who enter this business think they are far more skilled than they actually are because they've won a Toastmasters' contest, have a degree in speech communications, or they're a trial lawyer or other professional who speaks. Keynote speaking is the secret weapon of large-scale success in this business, and it's the most misunderstood medium. If you've never had professional level keynote speech training, I promise that you don't understand how it works. Once you're a successful keynoter and have a great content platform, you're ready to hire a publicist. I would recommend you hire someone year-round and make publicity a major part of your marketing.

You've been on Good Morning, America, The Today Show, BBC, NBC, FOX, CNN, HLN, and the Golf Channel, just to name a few. What's the key to getting on these big shows?

A good message that challenges conventional wisdom, adequate TV skills and presence, and a great publicist.

You seem to be in the media on all sorts of different subjects. You've been interviewed on Tiger Woods, debated executives over McDonald's and obesity, and have been quoted on the front-page of one of England's most-read newspapers calling the Prime Minister fat. Do you look for any topic to apply your message to?

Yes. My expertise is mental toughness and critical thinking, and I'll comment about anything that I can apply that expertise to.

You have to stay up on the news!

I read three newspapers a day, and my publicist reads more than that. Together, we don't miss many stories to comment on.

You've talked about some controversial issues in the media. Is that what they're looking for?

 Yes.

 Do you have to be an author to get in the media?

 No, but it helps.

 You've written some very controversial books. Has that made it easier for you to get in the media?

 Yes.

 Is that part of the reason you make them controversial and come up with titles like Die Fat or Get Tough?

 Yes.

Should speakers focus on positioning their books and materials in a way that the media will be interested in featuring?

Only if it fits their core message. You have to maintain the integrity of the message or you're simply selling out to the media. I refuse to do that. I've had multiple offers to star and co-star in reality shows in Hollywood and to be involved in other salacious media opportunities, and I've turned them all down.

At what point in your career did you start trying to get in the media?

Seven years after launching my career.

Do you wish you had done it earlier?

No, I wasn't ready and my message wasn't sharp or different enough. I was saying the same things as other speakers, and as a result I wouldn't have garnered much media attention.

Does being interviewed on TV require a different skill? Did you seek out separate training on how to be interviewed?

Yes. I was trained by a media expert who specializes in doing national television interviews. That's the key to success in this business. You need to hire the best people to train and prep you. If you want to be a serious player in this industry, you need to have a team of coaches to train you.

It seems as if a speaker is serious about getting in the media, they have to be willing to spend money and make an investment. For a person who is breaking into the business, at what stage should they plan to make this investment?

It's critical that you launch your career in stages. Publicity comes down the road when you are a successful speaker and author ready to move to the next level. The biggest mistake that new speakers make is moving too fast into areas in which they are not trained. Keynote speech training followed by a number of civic club speeches to hone your skills. Content development and sales process training. Media is a few years away for a new speaker.

What comes first: getting big as a speaker and then being featured in the media? Or getting big in the media and then becoming a big speaker?

Training and practicing to become a successful speaker is the first priority, followed by going out there and doing it. Then comes the media.

Any other thoughts on media in the speaking business?

Marketing is a critical aspect of the speaking business, and the combination of being a national keynote speaker and a thought leader in the media is the most effective strategy I've ever seen.

SUMMARY:

This chapter demonstrates the difference in thinking between most speakers and top speakers. I think most people look at this business in a very linear way. The linear way of looking at the media would be to think about how many books and speeches you can sell from people seeing you on TV. If I spend $10,000 a month on a publicist but only sell an extra $600 in books, some would argue that it's not worth the investment. On the other hand, looking at from a non-linear perspective, the $10,000 monthly investment is worth every penny. If I get in the media, it positions me as an authority on my topic. Being introduced as a speaker who has been featured on *Good Morning, America* and the *Today Show* naturally builds credibility, and that is the currency in this business. It's about people thinking they should listen to you. The more you can leverage the media, the more credible you will appear. There are two words that summarize the importance of media: implied endorsement. When you can say you've been featured on news stations and talk shows around the country, in the eyes of the public, there is a transfer of credibility from the show to the individual. While the stations aren't endorsing the speaker, in the eyes of the public, they think of the speaker and the media and think this person must be a big deal.

I'm still surprised that more speakers aren't leveraging the media. I've come to a few conclusions.

One: Most speakers are struggling to keep their doors open and the last place they want to allocate money is in a publicist who may or may not get them in the media and whose return on investment is neither guaranteed nor predictable.

Two: Speakers love to do everything on their own. I think speakers are very open to being in the media and would love the opportunity to be on major talk shows; however, they are not willing to pay for a publicist to do it. There are free resources out there, like www.helpareporter.com, where speakers can try to get in articles.

Three: I've come to realize you really have to be a thought leader and someone who is willing to take a stand on an issue or topic that very few people do. Steve is a great example. The media loves his book *Die Fat or Get Tough*. They love it because it is different than every other weight loss and diet book.

Don't underestimate the power of the media. I've seen what it has done for Steve over the past four years and if you leverage it the right way, it can be powerful and profitable.

BOOKS

 When did you write your first book?

 2005.

 By that point, you were already making over a million dollars?

 Yes.

 Why did you wait so long?

 Larry Wilson and other top speakers advised me to sell a $300 Mental Toughness workbook to the sales teams I was consulting as opposed to a $20 book. They also wanted me to sharpen my message so the book would stand out.

Did you have the urge to write it sooner?

 Oh, yeah. And most other speakers were telling me I needed a book to use as a marketing tool. I said this to Larry Wilson, and he told me that if I wanted to get the attention of major corporate executives, the book would have to not only be good and well written, but different than my competition. And he was right. Most speakers write their first book too early and are subsequently relegated to only working in the public market.

 When you finally got the okay, how long did it take you to write it?

 About eighteen months.

 I see many marketers telling speakers they can write a book in thirty days. Is this realistic and good advice?

 It's terrible advice, but it sells to new speakers who don't know better.

Does the book really have to be good?

Only if you want to be taken seriously by sophisticated buyers.

Is it smart to write a book so you can call yourself an author and use it as a business card?

Not if it's a bad book or one that says the same thing all the others on your topic do.

Do most speakers give away their books for free?

Yes. The average speakers sells 250 books and ends up giving the rest away because they can't sell them.

Do corporate executives who hire you read your books?

Yes, but that's because I'm a national convention keynoter. No executive is going to risk putting you onstage at their national convention without knowing your philosophy.

Did you write your books a certain way knowing they'd be reading it?

 Yes. My first five books were all written with 200-300 word chapters designed to make them friendly for an executive to read quickly. I purposely didn't include stories because high-level executives want to read content.

 When you finally finished your book, was it an instant success?

 Yes, we pre-sold thousands of copies to our database before I ever wrote a single word. We sold out of the first printing in eighty-two days.

 How many copies did you sell?

 About 130,000 copies

 Is that typical?

 Not for speakers.

It seems like most speakers who publish a book have no one to sell it to, and they end up having a big stack of books in their garage collecting dust and giving them away to family and friends. Is this usually because they're bad books or the lack of a database to sell them to?

Both. They go to NSA or some others speakers meeting and someone sells them on the idea that they have to have a book before they start speaking. So they spend all this time and money writing and publishing their book, and then they say, "Uh, oh. Who am going to sell this too?"

How many people did you have in your database when you sold your first book?

Twelve thousand.

Do you recommend having a certain size database before speakers write their first book?

Yes, I would have at least 1,000 people following you and your material before writing a book.

Since you released your first book in 2005, how many books have you sold?

 About 200,000.

 Do you think you would have sold as many books if you'd written them before you were big in the business and had a database?

 No.

 You call your book a best seller. It seems like authors are pretty liberal with this phrase. What does "best seller" mean to you?

 A best-selling book in this industry is 10,000 copies sold or more.

 Are your books still selling today?

 Seven days a week.

That has to be a nice extra stream of income.

We've earned over three million dollars in profits from my books.

Did you self-publish or go with a publisher?

I've had offers from major publishers on all of my books, but I've turned them down to maintain ownership of my intellectual property. This gives me the power to sell foreign rights and create derivative products and programs based on the book.

What are the pros and cons of each?

The pros of selling to a publisher are getting an advance on royalties as well as bookstore distribution, not to mention the bragging rights of having a mainstream publisher.

Did you think about accepting a traditional publisher's offer?

Sure, but only because it was a seven-figure offer.

What made you ultimately decide to do it on your own?

 They backed out due to the economic crash. It was bad timing.

 Looking back, are you glad you self-published?

 Oh, yes.

 Do you think you'd ever go with a big publisher?

 If the advance was large enough.

 In your opinion, what's the future of books?

 Digital and print on-demand.

Are speakers going to be able to profit as much?

Only if they understand that the profit is not in the book but in the intellectual property inside it. Intellectual property (IP) can be repackaged and sold in multiple mediums and formats.

You've appeared on some of the biggest TV shows in the world. Does being an author help?

Yes.

Your picture is on the front of most of your books. This goes against advice from major publishers. Why put it there?

Because the speaking business is built and grown on credibility, and our company's product is me.

Looking back, are you glad you listened to your mentors and waited to write your first book?

That one piece of advice made me a millionaire.

After writing five books, what's the most valuable lesson you've learned?

 Take your time and write the very best book you're capable of.

 Any other advice for speakers thinking of writing a book?

 Develop your speaking skills first and make sure you are saleable. Ignore the people who say you must have a book to speak. Build a database of fans before you write a word so you have someone to sell your book to.

SUMMARY

Many of the speakers I've talked to have either written a book or are in the process of writing one. Yet when I ask what their topic is, they say they're still working on it. Doesn't it seem a little strange to write a book before you really have your platform and point of view down? Speakers challenge me on this claiming that friends and family have urged them to write a book since they have a great story to share. It feels good to have this support, but I challenge them to think how much more successful their book could be if they actually had a 1,000 people on their database. You're more likely to make a profit if you have a following.

Another reason to wait until you have a fan base is so you can write the book based on what they're looking for. By speaking first, you will hear from the audience what they want to learn more about. For instance, this book is a product of all the feedback and questions I received over the past year. I discovered that speakers wanted to learn Steve's story about how he made it to the top as well as his views on different aspects of the business. It would have been way more challenging to have asked the questions in this book without learning the mindset of the aspiring speaker and the questions they ask.

A big difference between Steve and the average speaker struggling to make it is how calculated he is in making sure his books serve a purpose. The typical speaker I talk to feels they need to crank out a book so they can call themselves an author. The purpose in doing this is so that they can establish more credibility as a speaker and make some money selling it in the back of the room. Steve, on the other hand, will write a book to fulfill multiple purposes.

Always ask yourself, "What is the purpose of this book?" Don't just write a book to write a book. Know what your purpose is, who your buyer is, and who you're going to sell it to.

MULTI-DIMENSIONAL

BUSINESS MODEL

What does the average speaker's business model look like?

Most have one or two revenue sources, usually from speaking and training fees.

Is this a good model?

It's a terrible model, because if you're not speaking or training you're out of business.

Are speakers who follow this model struggling right now?

Except for the speakers with the highest fees, they've always struggled. Now many of them are going broke.

How is your business model different? What does it look like?

We have fifteen revenue streams every month, so whether I'm speaking or sleeping I'm making money.

What do you call this model?

It's a multidimensional business model.

What about the speakers in the Million Dollar Speakers' Group? Do most of them have a similar business model?

Yes, they are some of the best business people in this industry.

Do many of the speakers in the Million Dollar Speakers' Group make over a million dollars just from speaking fees?

 Most of them earn in excess of a million dollars per year in speaking-related income, which includes any revenue source driven through speaking.

 Is making over a million from speaking fees just too hard or do the million- dollar speakers not like the business model?

 Giving 100 or more speeches every year requires at least 250 days on the road, which can be brutal. All of us are capable of doing this but choose a better business model.

 It seems like some people enjoy only delivering the keynote speech and are not interested in training and consulting. For someone charging $15,000 a speech, they'd have to deliver 67 speeches a year to make over a million bucks. For someone charging$5,000, they'd have to deliver over 200 speeches. Do many people do this?

 Not unless they're celebrities. There are a few, but not many.

When you're delivering a keynote speech, what is your goal/ objective?

 To fulfill the contract, make the buyer happy, and gain interest in a training/consulting contract.

 Do you care more about the standing ovation or the economic buyer approaching you after the speech about other services you can provide?

 Standing ovations say more about the audience than the speaker. A fresh audience on Monday morning may stand and cheer and that same audience on Friday after a weeklong convention may sit on their hands. It's more about how they feel at that moment than the quality of the speech. As long as the customer is happy, I'm happy. What I'm looking for after that is the follow-up contract.

 Because of this, do you approach your speech differently than the average speaker who cares more about the standing ovation?

 Yes. Every keynote speech I deliver is written word for word and laced with stories and examples designed to pique the interest of the economic buyer in the audience.

You have a relatively small client list compared to most speakers. Does this have something to do with your business model?

Yes. My average client is a $30 billion dollar multinational corporation. Once I break into a company, my average stay is three to five years. My goal is to speak, train, and consult for every division, region, and area in every company I work with, and that adds up to hundreds of potential clients within each company and tens of millions of dollars in sales.

Where did you learn how to do this?

I learned it from the genius of the corporate market, the great Larry Wilson.

What is the role of training?

Training is preparation for long-term consulting.

What about consulting?

 Consulting is about getting serious long-term results.

 How many streams of income do you have coming in from your speaking business?

 Fifteen.

 How many of these streams first begin with the keynote?

 All of them are either driven or enhanced by my keynote.

 Is this why you spend so much time focusing on the keynote?

 Yes.

Where do you make most of your money?

 Consulting.

 Why do you focus on the keynote, then?

 The keynote gives you the rock star status you need to command world-class training and consulting fees.

 How often do you get a training or consulting contract from a speech?

 About 80% of the time.

 Which do you enjoy most: keynote, training, coaching, or consulting?

 I enjoy all of them, but the consulting is where you get the biggest results.

Which is the hardest to do?

The keynote, because doing it at the world-class level requires massive preparation and practice. Being a national keynote speaker is a pressure-packed profession. You literally have the success of the convention in your hands and millions of dollars of follow-up business on the line.

You charge $20,000 for six-hour training. I talk to trainers all the time who can only charge $2,000. They're always shocked at how much you can charge. Are you that much better than them?

Probably not.

Then why can you charge so much more?

Because I'm known as a national keynote speaker. In other words, I speak almost exclusively at national conventions for the biggest companies in the country. That gives me serious credibility. I'm also interviewed on TV, radio, and in business publications five hundred times per year all over the globe, which adds to my credibility as a world-class expert.

Which requires the most skill: speaking, training, or consulting?

 The keynote speech is the toughest and carries the most pressure.

 Which positions you the best?

 The keynote.

 Do you market yourself as a speaker, trainer, coach, consultant, or all four?

 I market myself as an expert in mental toughness training.

 Which can you make the most money with?

 In the long run, consulting is the most profitable, but it's usually the national convention keynote that gets you there.

Is your business model different for the public and corporate markets?

Completely. They are two different businesses.

If someone is already a successful trainer or consultant and feels comfortable speaking in front of people, will it be an easy transition to becoming a keynote speaker?

No. Being a national keynote speaker is much more difficult and detailed than most people think. It's the hardest thing I've ever done.

Do most organizations you work with ask what other services you provide other than the keynote?

Only if I use a layered sales approach in my speech, which is something very few speakers do or even know how to do.

Do you think they're usually looking for someone who can provide them with more than one service?

They are looking to solve problems and for experts who can help them.

Does this give you an advantage over other speakers during the selection process?

Absolutely.

For someone who wants to be a speaker and build a multidimensional business model, what should they focus on first?

The keynote speech.

Then what?

Getting good at the keynote speech and building a training and consulting program.

Any other advice for speakers as they're developing their business model?

Make sure you have tested your keynote, training, and consulting program before you sell it. You're only going to get one shot with a corporate buyer.

SUMMARY

The average speaker's business model consists of giving speeches. I think this is why so many speakers struggle because if they're not giving a speech or have one lined up, in a sense, they're out of business. When you look at the top speakers in this industry who own all the money, their business model is extremely different. A speaker like Steve, for example, goes into a company and gives a keynote speech. He cares less about the standing ovation and more about the economic buyer coming up to him after and saying, "Steve, I heard how you helped another company do this. Could you help us do that?"

Steve says, "I'm glad you asked." Now he goes back and does a one day training. All he's really doing there is saying, "Hey, guys, if you want bottom line results, you're not going to get it from a one day training."

Now they hire him back for a yearlong consulting deal where he can really help them increase their bottom line. The consulting is where Steve makes most of his money. The reason he gets hired for the training and consulting, and the reason he can charge the high fees that he does, all stems back to the positioning the keynote gives him. It positions him as a personality speaker. The company wants him and no one else.

Most speakers I've talked to after they've listened to Steve talk about multidimensional business models want to learn more and start implementing the model into their own business. It's fantastic that they see the potential with this model. But I always warn them, don't put the cart in front of the horse. Focus on the keynote first. As Steve mentioned, he can trace almost every stream of income he has back to the keynote. Once you have your speech down, people will approach you wanting more. Then you start building it for them.

One of the biggest mistakes people getting into this business make is not positioning their content correctly. They put content in their keynote that should be in their training, and vice versa. That's why most speakers earn so little money. They're not producing something organizations actually pay for. Get educated so that you know what content should be in your keynote, training, and consulting. 90% of people I've talked to over the past year have their content in the wrong place. It's costing them the opportunity to take their business to the next level because they're not producing what organizations pay for.

NSA/TOASTMASTERS/SSN

 When you first decided you wanted to become a speaker, where did you go?

 I joined a Toastmasters' club in Florida. I had studied speech in college, so between the two, I figured it would be enough training

 It seems like most people go to Toastmasters.

 They have 250,000 members.

 Is this a good organization?

 It's a great organization. It helps people overcome the fear of speaking and teaches them basic presentation skills.

When did you first become a Toastmaster?

 1996.

 What was your first impression of the organization?

 I was impressed.

 Was it good practice for you?

 Yes and no. It was good in the sense that it got me up in front of an audience once a week. It was bad in the sense that what they teach you at Toastmasters will not get you hired as a professional speaker.

 Is it a good place for most speakers to start?

 Not really, because if you want to get paid to speak you're going to have to unlearn most of the techniques you learn at Toastmasters. I'd rather see a new speaker get professional keynote speech training and later join Toastmasters to practice what they know will sell.

 Who do you recommend to Toastmasters?

 A professionally trained keynote speaker at the beginning of his or her career, or someone not interested in speaking professionally.

 Did you compete in the competitions?

 No.

 Maybe you should go back and try now?

 I'd probably lose!

Why didn't you compete?

I was trying to make money speaking, not win trophies.

If you can win competitions, does it mean you have the talent to be a fee paid professional speaker?

It has nothing to do with it. Toastmasters' champions are known for dramatic delivery and basic content, which is one of the reasons they win. Corporate buyers don't pay for that. They pay for world-class speaking skills combined with problem-solving content. Winning Toastmasters' contests is not the road to professional speaking.

Do very many of the speakers who win championships go on to become million-dollar speakers?

No.

What did you take away from being a Toastmaster?

Some good friends and memories. I enjoyed it. I'm still a member of the Bill Gove Golden Gavel Club in Florida. I attend whenever get a chance.

So Toastmasters doesn't provide the training speakers need to become professional speakers?

No, nor do they claim to.

Was Bill Gove ever big in Toastmasters?

No.

But he received the Golden Gavel Award, which is their highest honor.

Yes, in 1991. He had a lot of respect for the Toastmasters organization.

How do people know when to move on from Toastmasters?

Once you have been trained in professional keynote speaking, you can stay with Toastmasters as long as you wish. You need to be trained first so you know what to work on and what to ignore when other Toastmasters offer advice during their evaluations. If you don't get training first, you're going to be confused with all the advice from other members.

It seems as if the next biggest organization is the National Speakers' Association?

Toastmasters is an amateur speaker's organization. NSA is a professional speakers association.

What are your thoughts on NSA?

Bill Gove, my late business partner, was the first President of NSA and mentored many of the biggest names in NSA history. I've been a member for fifteen years and hold their highest earned designation, the CSP. I was honored to be named chairman of NSA's Million Dollar Speaker Group in 2011. I recommend NSA, but you have to understand that most of the members are struggling speakers, and you have to be very careful taking their advice.

What was it like going to NSA events with Bill?

It was like being with a rock star. I remember attending my first national convention with him in California. We're walking through the hotel lobby and this elderly speaker comes running up to Bill like a little kid seeing his hero. He thanked Bill again and again for his mentorship in the business and went on about how much it had helped him. The speaker was Zig Ziglar.

Was Bill Gove well known among NSA speakers?

Yes, and he was probably the most respected speaker in the association. Cavett Robert, the founder of NSA told me that there would be no NSA without Bill Gove.

I've attended an NSA national convention with you and seen NSA speakers up on stage talking about how to be successful in the speaking business. Yet, I don't think they're that successful themselves. How do you know who to listen to?

That's a very important question. I was lucky because I had Bill Gove to guide me. Everyone should have a mentor at the top of the business to help them separate the truth for the hype. And this business is full of hype.

Did Bill tell you whom to listen to?

 He actually made a list of twenty people.

 Would you ignore what everyone else had to say?

 Yes.

 Why?

 Because Bill told me that most people who attend the NSA conventions are struggling speakers.

 What would you and Bill do at most of the conventions?

 Walk the halls and talk to the most successful speakers. They would always find Bill.

Do you have any stories from attending conventions with him?

 The best stories I heard I couldn't repeat, because they involve inside information about the industry. It was an education you can't buy. It's where I learned the good, bad, and ugly about the business. It armed me with information that's been invaluable. As they say in New Jersey, I know where all the bodies are buried. I know the serious speakers from the pretenders, and there are lots of pretenders in NSA.

 NSA awards designations. Is it important for speakers to have designations?

 Only if you want to be recognized in NSA. The clients couldn't care less.

 Why is there such an emphasis on them among speakers?

 There's a lot of ego in this business, and speakers love to impress one another. The best description I've ever heard of professional speakers came from a fellow member at an NSA convention. I forget her name, but I never forgot what she said: "Speakers are ego-maniacs with inferiority complexes." She was being funny, but there's a lot of truth in that.

Why do you use CSP behind your name?

I'm an ego-maniac with an inferiority complex!

Seriously though

I use it because I'm not well known in NSA, and speakers think it's a big deal. The truth is I know lots of CSP's who are broke in the business. The most difficult thing about getting the CSP is the five years of paperwork

I've heard corporate executives say they have no idea what those designations mean. Do you think you get hired because you have a CSP?

I've never been hired from having a CSP and don't know anyone that has.

I've contacted several CSPs about joining SSN and they've always asked me what other CSPs are involved. Why is this? Does CSP mean you're extremely successful?

You can earn a schoolteacher's income and be a CSP, but most people don't know that. They buy into these designations that mean nothing in terms of success. Tell me you're a CSP and all it tells me is you have delivered some speeches, have some clients, and are persistent with paperwork. Tell me you won the CPAE Hall of Fame award and all that tells me is your politically connected in NSA. Tell me you're a member of NSA's Million Dollar Speakers' Group and you've earned my respect and attention. That's the only NSA group that represents serious financial success in this business.

Can you be successful in the speaking business and not have a CSP?

Most of wealthiest speakers in this business that I know don't have the CSP. What they do have is money.

Is NSA more of an educational organization or an organization for speakers to do business?

It's an educational trade group that caters to new and struggling speakers.

Have you generated business from being a member of NSA?

No. But the connections I've made in the Million Dollar Speakers' Group have been valuable.

Have you received referrals?

I have paid referral relationships with other members, but they were not developed at NSA.

You were the 2011 chairman of the National Speakers Association Million Dollar Speaker Group. What is this group?

It's a very small group of NSA speakers who can prove they've earned at least one million dollars in speaking revenue in the past 12 months. You have to qualify every year. I've been a member since its inception.

Is it a big group?

In 2012, we had 39 members worldwide, out of 5,000 total NSA members.

What are some things members of this group are doing that the average speaker is not?

 I spoke to the general session at last year's NSA convention detailing the five differences between the average NSA speaker and the Million Dollar Speakers, and these are the five differences I cited: 1. They treat their business like a business, not a hobby. 2. They sell processes over programs. 3. They are thought leaders, not thought followers. 4. They have a multidimensional business model. 5. They focus on making money, not getting standing ovations.

 As part of being the 2011 chairman, you've traveled around to different state's NSA chapters. What advice do you give?

 I try to help the new and struggling speaker approach their business more strategically. Most speakers fail to recognize that the speaking business operated at the highest level is based on leverage, not running around giving as many speeches as possible. This business is different than any other business I've ever seen, and most people struggle or fail in it because they try to apply strategies from the industry they come from to this industry.

 Are there any other speakers groups out there besides NSA and Toastmasters?

 SSN is the only paid referral network in the business. If you're looking for referrals and you have a solid speech or training program, you should join.

Do you recommend speakers be part of NSA?

Yes, as long as you know what it is and what it's not, and that most of the speakers are struggling and will gladly offer you bad advice. They are well intentioned and nice people, but few of them understand how the money flows in this business.

What should they expect to learn and not learn from being a member?

You can expect to learn a lot of little details from some very smart people. It will help your business and you'll enjoy the friends you make. What you won't learn much about is how to make serious money. There are very few people inside or outside of NSA who know how to earn big money in this business, and those are the people you must get to know. Find a million-dollar speaker and follow everything he/she tells you, whether he/she is in NSA or not.

Do you have any other thoughts on NSA, Toastmasters, or other speaking groups?

I'm pro-NSA, Toastmasters, and SSN. You just have to know how to use each of them to enhance your career. Used correctly, they all have value.

SUMMARY

I've never seen Steve get more heat from people than when he talks about speakers' groups. I remember him calling me late on a Saturday night after he'd attended a speakers' meeting. He was sitting next to one of the biggest speakers in the business (you would know the name) and they were listening to a speaker talk about how they should market themselves. Afterwards, the meeting planner asked Steve what he thought of the meeting. Steve was blunt and said he was not impressed. He told the planner that he didn't understand why he was sitting next to one of the highest grossing, most well-known speakers of all time and listening to someone talk about marketing who is an amateur in this business. The meeting planner was offended. He told Steve you should let everyone have a chance to share their information and that all the attention should not be on the top speakers. I get it. But when it comes to learning, who do you want to learn from? I used to play hockey. If I was at a one-day event on how to shoot a puck and was learning from the number one high school hockey player while one of the top NHL players of all time, Wayne Gretzky, was sitting next to me, you can bet I'd be disappointed, too.

When I first decided I wanted to speak, I Googled speakers' associations and came across NSA. I remember seeing the speaker designations and thinking that if I wanted to be a big speaker, I needed to have one. The more I've learned about this business, the less necessary I've learned they are. I've had a few speakers tell me their first focus is to join a speakers' group and get a designation so that they have credibility marketing themselves as a speaker. From the executives I've talked to, they could care less what designations you have as long as you can solve their problem. If having other aspiring speakers look up to you is important, get the designation. But know that it's not going to pay the bills.

Here are my thoughts on the three speakers' organizations:

Toastmasters is a fantastic organization. It has helped so many people, especially business people, become more comfortable getting up and speaking in front of people. That being said, Toastmasters does not produce million-dollar speakers. I've said that to Toastmaster governors and presidents and they all agree. If you're not looking to become a professional speaker and simply want a place to learn how to feel more comfortable speaking, Toastmasters is a dynamite resource. As Steve mentioned, if you're professionally trained, this can be a great place to test your material. You can learn more by visiting www.toastmasters.com

The National Speakers Association is by far the largest organization in the professional speaking business and a great place to connect with other speakers. There are meetings in every state, and there is a national convention every year. From the members I've talked to and from my own observations, this is a great group to be a part of if you want to meet other speakers. This group will not provide the training you need to be a top speaker. If it did, there would be more successful speakers in it. Learn more by visiting www.nsa.org.

The Siebold Success Network is unlike the other groups in that its primary purpose is to generate more business for its members. This is the group that can literally give a speaker the break they are looking for. For the speaker just starting and learning the business, the downside is that it may take some time to generate new business since they'll have to build trust among referral agents. The upside is that new speakers can start building relationships with referral agents around the world so that when they are ready to make their break, they already have an army of people ready to refer them. You can learn more by visiting www.ssnlive.org.

All three groups are great. Just know the purpose of each one and what you expect to get out of it.

PRODUCTS

Do most speakers sell products?

Successful speakers with large databases, which are a small percentage of speakers, do. Many speakers have books and products, but very few speakers sell their products. The average speaker sells 250 copies of their book and even fewer copies of their recordings. The rest are sitting in garage collecting dust.

Is this a profitable part of most speaker's businesses?

Only for the speakers who actually sell them.

Give me some examples of products speakers sell in the business?

 Books, CD's, DVD's, Membership Websites, etc.

 How do you come up with products?

 I create products based on what my fan base is interested in and what I'm excited about.

 Do you beta test them?

 I used to when my database was smaller. Today it's large enough to move most any product I write or record.

 How do you know how to price them?

 We test various price points based on competitive products from other speakers.

What is your philosophy on products? Do they have to be good?

They have to be great or the customer will never trust you again.

Does your product have to be proven?

If you're new in the business, you have to prove everything you do. After you build a large enough following, people trust your products.

Do you focus on selling people what they need or what they want?

Good question. Over three thousand speakers call our office every year asking for advice on their careers, and we always recommend that they get professional training in the Bill Gove Speech Workshop. That's what all of them need, yet most of them believe all they need is help with marketing. These people have no idea how good you have to be to make it in this business, and there are plenty of manipulative marketers who will sell them on the idea that this is an easy business. So many times, they will skip the keynote speech training for the sexier alternative of speaker marketing. 99.9 % of these people never make it because they are marketing an inferior product, which is their speaking skill. The only people who benefit are the marketers, and there are new speakers for them to sell every day. I'm proud of the fact that we tell people the truth about what it really takes to make it in this business, even though it's cost us a fortune doing it. By the time a new speaker figures out that we were telling them the truth while the slick speaker marketers were lying to them, it's usually too late and they have wasted thousands of dollars. It's sad, but true.

 At what point should a speaker start creating products?

 When they have a large enough database to sell them to. It takes years to develop that big of a following.

 What are some good first products a speaker should focus on?

 Build a process that helps people make positive changes. Whether it's a coaching program, consulting process or multi-day seminar, build a program that gives people the skills they need to succeed.

 What are the margins like for products in the speaking business?

 Very high, north of 90% on most products besides books.

Are most speaker products short-lived or are many of them timeless?

It depends on the topic. Technology for example, is always changing. But most personal growth products are timeless, and they will sell for twenty to thirty years if they are really good.

This can be a nice extra stream of passive income.

A good speaker with a large database can earn millions in product sales.

Can you create products yourself?

I've recorded at Nightingale-Conant and other major studios, but with the advances in technology, I record almost everything in my home studio. It's cost-effective, convenient, and the sound quality is phenomenal.

You've put out lots of products over the years. Is there a common theme among the products that have been successful?

Not really. Some have sold more than others. I wish I knew the magic formula, but I don't. I just try to over-deliver and serve my fan base the best I can. I never release a substandard product, and it's been a very profitable part of our business.

What about the ones that have failed?

The products that have failed have been the ones that require serious effort from the listener/viewer. Most people will listen to a recording or watch a video, but few are willing to take action on the information. Most people are better dreamers than doers, and products or programs that require action by the customer are usually the ones that fail.

Have you lost money on products before?

Not on books, audio, or video recordings, but we've lost money on programs. One was a program called Public Speaking Idol, which was a contest to find the next great speaker in America. We invested about $25,000 building the website and promoting it. It was a total bomb. I'm still not sure why, but we only had about one hundred people sign up for it. That was our worst program failure.

What mistake do most speakers make when they lose money on products?

The biggest mistake is they record their product far too early in their career before they have really honed their craft and sharpened their message. The second mistake is they create a product with no one to sell it to. Many new speakers are sold on the idea that the first thing they should do is write a book or record a product, which is the dumbest thing you can do. It sells because it's sexy, while getting training and working on your speech every day is not. People who sell marketing to speakers know exactly what they want to hear, and they profit from selling misinformation. New speakers are duped into buying things they don't need, the most common is writing a book and recording audios and videos. They just don't know any better, and it's too bad. That's why this book is so important, and I applaud you for writing it. You're telling the truth about this business, and I'm proud to be a part of it.

 Are there certain products that sell better in the public market than in the corporate market and vice versa?

Yes. Books sell well in corporations. Books, audio materials, and videos sell well in the public market.

Public seminars seem like a great way to teach information. Are these profitable?

 They can be very profitable. They are also extremely risky.

 Do most speakers make money putting on public seminars?

 90% of public seminars lose money.

 Why is this?

 They overspend on sales and marketing, overestimate the number of attendees, and end up paying for guarantees on empty hotel rooms.

 Do you draw the line on how much you'll spend marketing a seminar?

 Yes. We never exceed 20% on sales and marketing costs. So if we are selling a $4,000 per person seminar, we won't spend more than $800 per person in sales and marketing expenditures.

I hear speakers say they're putting on a seminar or workshop. What's the difference?

Seminars are larger and more content driven. Workshops are smaller, interactive, and more expensive.

Do you pre-sell tickets before you confirm the event? Is this one of your strategies to make sure you're always in the black?

We used to do this when our database was smaller. It's a good idea when you're getting started. It's a solid method of mitigating your risk.

You're one of the rare speakers out there who actually puts on a profitable public seminar. Why do you think you've been so successful?

We really stick to a series of formulas that work. They include the 20% sales and marketing maximum, minimizing financial exposure with hotel room guarantees, and effective pricing strategies. It's a tough business, but if you're careful and calculated, you can earn millions. The secret is not to try to break the bank on every seminar, and it's easy to get greedy. There are speakers who have made more money in public seminars than we have, but I don't know any who have never lost money. After conducting hundreds of public seminars over the past sixteen years, we have never lost money. We've made as much as $250,000 and as little as $9,000 in profit, but we never lose money. I recommend being cautious and highly trained before you attempt this aspect of the business. The best way to learn is to sell for someone else. In twelve months, you'll understand why so many speakers lose money and a lot more about how to be profitable. It's a very tricky.

What do you predict the future entails for speaker's products?

With the popularity of resources like YouTube, Google, and others that distribute free content, speakers are being forced to create more unique products people can't get for free, and it's weeding out the middle class of this business. This is the best thing that could have happened to the business, because it's pushing us to offer better solutions. For the speakers who rise to the occasion, it's the chance of a lifetime. I'm personally looking forward to the challenge and fully intend on earning millions more in product sales.

It seems like speakers are giving more things away for free. What are your thoughts on this?

I believe in giving away promotional products like speech clips, TV interview segments, and copies of articles, and even free courses. We even offer a ten-day course called FreeSpeakingCourse.com, which over 50,000 people have taken. We offer another free course called Fatloser.com to help people lose weight. The idea is to offer people the opportunity to sample your style and content with no risk. If they like it, they will become fans and probably purchase your products and attend your seminars in the future. It's all about being flexible in a fluid marketplace.

Anything else in regard to products?

 Don't fall into the trap of writing a book or creating products before you have a differentiated message and adequate fan base. Be smart and get the proper training you will need to deliver a professional quality speech. Take the right steps in the correct order and you will build a successful career without wasting money. Beware of people who tell you that you can't succeed as a speaker without a book. I was earning well over a million dollars a year before I ever had a book, because I was coached by the best in the business. By the time my first book came out, it became a best seller almost immediately selling over 100,000 copies. The reason was simple: my message had been refined over years of speaking to groups and seeing what they respond to. This business is a marathon, not a sprint. Avoid the get-rich-quick mentality, and you'll build a solid business that will boomerang your message around the world and give you and your family a lifestyle most people only dream of.

SUMMARY

If there is one thing you take away from this chapter, I hope it's this: the one and only product you should be focusing on is YOU. This is a personality-driven business where YOU are the product. Until you have a world-class product (you delivering a world-class keynote speech), you have nothing to market and sell. Turn yourself into a world-class keynote speaker, and you will have a following who will want to buy every different kind of product you create.

Several speakers have told me they know they need training in order to go to the next level, yet they don't have the money. So they use the money they have to create a product in hopes that by selling the product, they'll make enough money to get training. The unfortunate part is that from all the people I've interviewed and talked with, I've never seen this work.

SALES

 How do you sell yourself for a speech?

 I sell a solution, which is mental toughness to enhance performance, develop people, and help them thrive through change.

 Who typically hires you to speak?

 National or regional vice presidents of large sales teams

 Why this person?

 I've always marketed myself as a mental toughness speaker to Fortune 500 sales teams, and VP's of sales run those teams.

Is it important to know who hires you?

It's critical. The more you know about the customer, the easier it is to sell him or her.

Do they usually have to get approval from someone else, or is this the decision maker you're targeting?

It's the decision maker.

In corporate, do you typically sell your services the first time you talk to an executive?

No.

How long is the average sales cycle in corporate?

Six to twelve months.

The follow-up must be pretty important?

It's very important. Follow-up is everything in this business.

You talk about building a pipeline. Explain what this is?

You want to build a pipeline of prospects, so you always have speeches and programs pending.

How many people do you like having in your pipeline?

I always have eight to ten deals pending at any given time.

Once you get a prospect in your pipeline, how often do you follow up?

As often as you can without being a pest. At least once a month.

Do you find that following up by phone or email works best?

 Phone.

 It seems like you're on the phone a lot in this business. How important is it to be comfortable selling and talking to people over the phone?

 It's huge. We do everything but deliver the speech over the phone.

 Do executives typically try to negotiate with you as you're selling your services?

 Not in the big companies.

 What groups or organizations typically want to negotiate?

 Small companies and associations.

When you get hired for a speech, how much advance notice do you get? Are you usually hired out a year in advance?

Before the great recession, the booking times were much longer. Now it's four to eight weeks on average.

Do organizations look for speakers at the last minute, or do they typically schedule them months or years in advance?

They schedule in advance.

Do you have a process for up-selling your products?

Yes. It's called layered selling. It's basically building subtle sales messages into the speech or training session.

How often does this work?

It works around 80% of the time, depending on the program.

When you're selling your programs, do executives want to talk to you? Or are they satisfied speaking to your Chief Operating Officer, Dawn Andrews?

 The executives talk to me, and their assistants talk to Dawn.

 Do most speakers have sales teams that sell them?

 No. Executives want to deal with the speaker directly.

 What are your thoughts on how a speaker is positioned when he or she cold calls a prospect? Does it position him or her well?

 Speakers that cold-call in this business aren't taken seriously by executives. This is a credibility-based business, and cold-calling isn't credible when you're selling a ten-thousand-dollar speech

 Is selling to a Fortune 500 executive different than selling to an owner of small company?

 It's very different. Corporate executives are the most sophisticated buyers in the business. They are the toughest to sell, but they also offer the most potential for long-term business.

Do you use a different sales strategy?

 Yes.

 Where did you learn how to sell to corporate executives?

 Larry Wilson and Bill Gove.

 For someone who doesn't have these connections, where can they learn how to sell to executives?

 We have a program called Corporate Speaker Sales School, and it's fantastic. It's the only program of its kind in the industry taught by a Fortune 50 executive?

 What are the biggest mistakes speakers make when selling their services?

 They focus on features instead of solutions, they talk too much and listen too little, and they assume they know the executive's problem.

Do speakers get stuck selling to the wrong person? Are they wasting time selling a person in an organization who can't write a check?

Yes. You need to speak directly to the economic buyer. Most others are a waste of time.

Whom do you like to sell to the most?

The person who can write the check for speaking, training, and consulting.

What is the biggest mistake you've made over the years selling your services?

Selling them on the benefits of my program before I clearly understood the executive's problem.

Is selling to the corporate vs. public market two different types of sales?

Completely different. The corporate market is much more difficult.

How does a speaker know whom to sell to? For example, if they want to speak to an association, how would they know who they should be calling or sending their material to?

It's typically the same level buyer in every group. The best way to learn is to ask people in the association, "Who is responsible for hiring speakers for your annual convention?" They will gladly tell you. It's not as easy in a corporation.

Do you need to be a good sales person to be able to sell your services?

Yes. Speakers need to learn how to sell themselves. Executives don't like dealing with anyone else.

Can you be a big speaker and not be good at sales?

Only if you're a celebrity. I honestly don't know a six- or seven-figure speaker who's not a competent sales person. I'm sure there are a few, but I don't know of any. Learning to sell in this business is critical for large-scale success.

For someone who is new in the business, describe what back-of-the-room sales (BOR) is?

The literal definition is selling your books and other products at the back of the room you're speaking in.

Which market can you use this with?

 The public market.

 Is back-of-the-room sales profitable?

 It can be very profitable.

 Have you made more in the back of the room than you have from your speaking fee?

 At times, when the audience was large enough.

 It seems as if there are different philosophies among speakers for selling from the back of the room. What are they?

 The selling strategies range from sophisticated to manipulative. You have to decide how you want to be known in the industry and to your fan base.

Which philosophy do you follow?

 I like to sell as though I'm advising a family member.

 What do you mean by that?

 I want them to get the best possible deal and only buy what they need.

 Do you follow this philosophy in all aspects of your business?

 Yes.

 Explain.

 I want to be known for being a straight shooter. I want my fans to trust me. I want to offer them my best advice, even if it costs me money.

Any other thoughts on selling in the speaking business?

I think you've got to believe in what you're selling, and then be aggressive and bold in the process. When it comes to mental toughness training, I believe I'm the best in the business. I'm not bragging; I actually believe it. I tell my clients that and then let them decide. There are times in this business where modesty is appropriate, but selling is not one of them.

SUMMARY

Notice how Steve answered the question about the average sales cycle for booking a corporate engagement. He said it can take around eight to ten months. I know this is accurate because, since working with Steve, I've heard of so many pending deals he has with corporate. They're all big deals that don't happen overnight. I highlight this point because I often hear speakers tell me they plan on quitting their job next month and start speaking. They don't understand our business or realize that it's not as easy as picking up the phone and getting an engagement, especially in corporate. I'd recommend keeping your job, and getting training so that you can be building your speech and working on your speaking skills while you're still making money. Once you have your speech down, you can start selling your services. When you get to the point of having too many engagements, then you're at a good point to transition.

Spend time learning the sales process. First, find out who the economic buyer is. Too many speakers have no idea who this is. They're wasting their time selling to someone who is not the decision maker. Second, know how to sell this person. If you plan on selling to corporate, you're up against some of the most sophisticated buyers. I've participated in the Corporate Speakers' Sales School, a training program for speakers to learn how to sell their services to executives. The executive running the course has torn apart script after script because it wasn't concise and strong enough. As an executive, she's going to give you three minutes on the phone. If you can't identify her problem and sell your service in three minutes, you're not going to get a second call. I consider myself a pretty good salesperson, but this is a whole different beast. I don't say this to intimidate speakers, only to demonstrate that this is a tough sale and you better be prepared and extremely polished if you're going to succeed.

I've talked to speakers who say they're horrible at sales. Their plan is to hire an agency to book them engagements. That's not how this business typically works. If you're trying to break in to the business and you're relying on someone else to get you engagements, I'd rethink your strategy or question who it is who you're listening to.

Don't downplay the importance of the sales process. Learn it. Study it. Practice it. And then get mentally tough and follow it.

TRAINING

 When you first started in the business, did you think you needed training?

 No. I was a speech major in college and a successful Toastmaster. I thought I was really good and just needed help marketing myself.

 Why did you think you were good enough to start without professional training?

 Because I was the best speaker in my speech classes in college and my friends at Toastmasters told me I was good enough to get paid.

 When did you realize you needed it?

 After losing fifty thousand dollars in my first year in business.

Where did you go looking for it?

I hired six different marketing consultants that were members of NSA.

How did you know who to listen to?

I didn't. They all seemed credible.

Why did you think they could help you?

They were very convincing.

How much were you spending?

Tens of thousands of dollars.

Knowing what you know now, is this typical?

 No, but I was speaking full time and I was trying to expedite the process.

 How much should speakers expect to pay in order to get professional training?

 It's not about what it costs. It's about what the training offers. New speakers don't need marketing advice until they are good enough to be marketed. Have you ever heard of a business where you build the marketing campaign before you develop the product?

 Did you think they were helping you at first?

 Yes, because they were telling me I was on the right track and I would be making money within months.

When did you realize it wasn't good advice?

 After blowing $50,000 and being no closer to my goal.

 Now we all know the story of how you met Bill Gove. Why did he tell you not to listen to anyone else in the business?

 Because this business is full of charlatans who will tell you it's an easy business and you don't even have to be a good speaker. There's big money in telling people how easy this business is, and new speakers don't know they're being lied to. Many speakers running marketing seminars are making fortunes telling speakers exactly what they want to hear, which is not to worry about their speaking skills and focus on marketing. They told me the same thing and I was naïve enough to believe it. The first thing Bill Gove told me to do was fire all six of them, which is exactly what I did.

 You lost fifty thousand listening to all these guys. Then you took the Bill Gove Speech Workshop. Did it teach you the same things you had learned from all these other speaker trainers?

 No, it was all about building my keynote speech. I had to unlearn almost everything I thought I knew about speaking. It was unbelievable. I was so excited to finally be on the right track under the guidance of a master. Little did I know what I was learning in those two days would make me a millionaire. I knew it was special, I just didn't know how special.

How was the BGSW different than all the other trainings?

The Bill Gove system was developed by one of the greatest keynote speakers who ever lived. Bill Gove was the father of the professional speaking industry. He delivered keynote speeches around the world alongside people like Ronald Reagan, Billy Graham, Napoleon Hill, and Norman Vincent Peale for over fifty years. This man was a giant, and he eventually trained more million-dollar speakers than any coach in history.

What did it teach you?

The finer details of what it takes to hold twenty thousand people in a sold-out stadium in the palm of your hands.

Did you learn things you didn't already know?

Oh, God. Yes! I had no idea what I needed to know to be successful as a keynote speaker. I didn't how good I was going to have to be in order to get paid to speak. I had listened to too many lies.

Do you feel like all the time you had spent before the workshop was a waste?

Yes. I wasted my first twelve months listening to nonsense from people who didn't know what they were talking about. They all claimed to know how to market me, yet none of them were marketing themselves. It was pure stupidity, and it still makes me angry because new speakers are still falling into the same trap. Selling marketing is sexy. Learning the craft of professional speaking is not. Guess which sells better to new speakers?

How long did it take you to start making money after you took the workshop?

I went from $500 a speech to $5,000 in thirteen months after attending the workshop.

How long does it take most people once they understand the business and have the training?

It varies, but most successful speakers take five to seven years to build a substantial speaking business. This is a serious skill that takes time to develop. No one does it overnight.

How soon can people implement the material they learn from the workshop?

Immediately. I learned the Bill Gove System and spoke to two hundred Rotary and Kiwanis clubs to hone my skills. When I finished, I started charging $5,000 per speech.

Do most million-dollar speakers get training along the way?

Yes, and many of them are Bill Gove graduates.

Is it that they weren't talented at the start or that they needed a better understanding of how the business works?

This business is more about skill than raw talent. Many new speakers are very talented but they don't possess the platform skills that companies pay for. Until you have professional platform skills, you have no speaking business. Any high school kid can deliver a book report or a Toastmasters' speech, but being paid requires world-class skill.

What do most aspiring speakers need training on? Is it their speaking skills? The business? Marketing?

Speaking skills come before anything else. We're not talking about public speaking skills; we're talking about professional speaking skills. The difference is measured in money.

When speakers are looking for training, what do you advise they ask about and look for?

The single most important question to ask about any speaking seminar or workshop is how successful their graduates have been. The success of the graduates defines any school, whether it's Harvard, Stanford, or Yale. Speakers need to do their homework and carefully vet the programs they're interested in.

There are many different speaker training programs out there. Are they all the same, or do they all teach something a little different?

Most of them teach basic presentation skills disguised as professional speaking skills. That's not what you want. New speakers should focus on learning the keynote speech, which is much different and more difficult than any other form of presentation. It's also the highest paid and most prestigious.

It seems like everybody who feels comfortable and confident speaking is some kind of speech coach. How do you really know whom to listen to?

 Look at who they've coached to success.

 What questions do you recommend that someone ask if they are going to hire a coach?

 Ask them one simple question: how many people that have attended your course have become million-dollar speakers? It's a fair question.

 It seems as if people can market themselves and look way bigger than they really are. How do you know the speaker is really what they say they are?

 Google them. Type in their name on YouTube and see what comes up. What is the press saying about them? Are they being interviewed on radio and television? If the press isn't interviewing them, they are probably not as big as you think. Don't read what they say about themselves. Read and watch what the media says. That will give you an unbiased view.

The Bill Gove Speech Workshop is known as the "Harvard of Professional Speaking Schools." Why does it have this reputation?

Harvard is famous for producing senators and presidents. The Bill Gove Speech Workshop is famous for producing million-dollar speakers.

Can you give me some examples of BGSW graduates?

Bob Proctor, the star of the hit movie, The Secret. Larry Wilson, the highest-grossing corporate speaker in history. Cavett Robert, the founder of the National Speakers' Association. Brian Tracy, Don Hutson, Nido Qubein, Jim Cathcart, Dr. Tony Alessandra. The list goes on and on. If you want to see more names, visit www.speechworkshop. com, and you can see many more of the million-dollar speaker graduates.

When you attended the Bill Gove Speech Workshop, it was one-on-one. You paid significantly more than the workshop costs today. Does the size of the class matter? Should it be one-on-one, or does it matter that there are 500 people in a room?

The size of the class is critical. Since it opened in 1947, The Bill Gove Speech Workshop has always limited the class size to twenty people or fewer. This allows everyone to deliver speeches during the workshop with plenty of time to be coached and get answers to their questions.

When Bill Gove passed away in 2001, what were his wishes for the workshop?

 That we would continue it with the same gold standard of quality in which he established and conducted it.

 Did he make you promise him anything?

 Yes, that we would eventually pass it down to the next generation who would fulfill the same promise. He knew that it was the best keynote workshop in the industry and he wanted to guarantee its long-term legacy.

 Do you enjoy coaching it?

 I love it. It's the one workshop in the industry where attendees are exposed to the good, bad, and ugly of this business. What we do here is important because the people who attend have a dream, and the only thing standing between them and their dream is good information and hard work. We tell them the truth, show them the system, and guide them to success. Just yesterday, Jason Forrest, another Bill Gove Graduate, became a million-dollar speaker at age thirty-three, only four years after attending the workshop. It's a great feeling to see people's dreams become reality. He is now a member of the most elite group of speakers in the world.

Is it a big part of your business?

No, but it's one of the most enjoyable.

How is the workshop conducted now?

In a small group format during a three-day weekend in different cities across the United States, England, and Australia.

Are the workshops big?

Twenty people or fewer.

Is there any kind of follow up?

Yes. There's a twelve-month marketing course included in the workshop. We have a private weekly email that goes out to all the graduates that keeps them up-to-date on events and gives them reminders of the Bill Gove System content. We also have a private Facebook page for the graduates to help them network with each other and promote their speaking dates, book releases, and media interviews. They even help each other book speaking dates. The Bill Gove Graduates are like one big family.

 You get calls from speakers all year looking for help. What's your best advice for people looking for training?

 It depends on what they want to do. If you just want to be a seminar leader, facilitator, or power point presenter, going to Toastmasters and practicing might be enough. If you want to be a rock star keynote speaker signing autographs in stadiums and being interviewed on radio and television, go to the Bill Gove Speech Workshop. It literally made my career and it may do the same for you.

SUMMARY

Please. If you're serious about this business, get training. I mean, real training, from someone who is in this business and successful. Don't fall prey to the mentality of the masses who try to learn this business on their own.

If I had the dream of becoming a basketball star and had the chance to be coached by Michael Jordan for one day, and it cost me $25,000, I'd do it in a heartbeat. If you're someone who doesn't think you need training, I'd have to challenge you for a second and ask how committed you are to becoming a speaker. What industry can you earn the kind of money Steve makes and not have training? Where can you make $15,000 in forty minutes? Maybe if you're a heart surgeon, professional athlete, musician, or actor. But these are all professions that require years of training. I've seen how hard the top speakers work and how much training they've gone through to perform at the highest level. They've worked hard and deserve the high fees they get paid. It's basic supply and demand. Few other speakers can do what they do. If you think you're going to walk into the business at the highest level and make a million dollars with no training, you're crazy. I've become close with several million dollar speakers and not one of them would say they did it without guidance and training from a bigger speaker. Yet, I've talked to over a thousand speakers this past year and I'd guess 90% of them don't think they need training. I know there can be a lot of ego in this business, but don't be delusional and think you're good enough to play in the big leagues without help. Get the training and do it the right way. When you do, you'll separate yourself from the masses and be able to play at a level very few speakers can even imagine.

MILLION-DOLLAR

SPEAKER LIFESTYLE

How would you describe the lifestyle of a million-dollar speaker?

It's like living a dream. It's doing what you want, when you want, with whom you want for as long as you want without ever having to answer to anyone else unless you wish. Its life at it's best. In the words of Ayn Rand, it's living an unrestricted existence

Describe your average day.

There are two types of average days. One is at home and the other is on the road.

At home, I get up around eight a.m., have breakfast, and study for whatever book I'm writing for about two hours. Then I head out on the boat and write on the lake for a couple of hours. At about one p.m., I pull into the dock, pick up my wife, and boat over to the country club for lunch. After that, we boat home and I work out for an hour in our home gym.

After the workout, I'll read for an hour or so and take a nap for about an hour to an hour and a half. I'll finish the day by doing corporate conference calls, speaker coaching calls, and return calls. I usually do at least one radio, newspaper, or magazine interview before the work day is over. At seven p.m., Dawn and I pour a drink and head back down to the boat to watch the sunset on Lake Lanier. It's majestic. We sit on the lake for a few hours recapping the business day and planning for the next. It's a very relaxing and rewarding lifestyle.

On the road is completely different. I usually wake up around five a.m. to prepare for my first TV interview of the morning. I'm often on two morning shows in whatever city I'm in. After the TV interviews, a limousine takes me to the hotel or arena where I'm delivering my speech. I'll sign autographs and take photos with audience members in the lobby before they open the doors, and then head backstage to meet with the company executives before I go onstage. I'll do my final rehearsal in the green room or backstage so I'm fresh when I go on. After the speech, I'm whisked to a private room where I'll meet with the local press and take photographs with the company's executives. Sometimes, they'll ask me to tape a short endorsement video of their company or product. After that, the limo takes me to the airport and I fly to the next city.

 Do you rehearse your material every day?

 When I'm preparing for a speech or a speaking tour I do one to two full word-for-word rehearsals every day, starting six weeks before the speech or tour.

If you book a speech, how many times do you rehearse that speech?

Once the speech is written word-for-word and I'm happy with it, I rehearse it about thirty times. By the time I hit rehearsal number ten, I could deliver the speech word-for-word in my sleep. The last twenty rehearsals are preparation for problems on stage. I pressure-proof every speech to be 100% sure I can deliver it flawlessly, no matter what happens on stage or in the audience and how much pressure I'm under.

That seems like more preparation than the average speaker I know. Did you learn that from someone or did you develop that habit yourself?

It is, and yes, I learned it from the great Bill Gove. He insisted on over-rehearsing every speech. He was the consummate professional.

How much time do you spend writing?

Two hours per day

Why two hours?

 After I study for two hours, I can write like a madman for two more and then I start getting sloppy. The two-hour time frame keeps me fresh and eager to write every day.

 Is this for books, speech material, or whatever you're working on at the time?

 It's usually for my next book, but sometimes I'll be in between books and writing sales copy or something else.

 How many hours a day to you spend studying?

 Two.

 How often do you read?

 Usually seven days a week. In this business you have to be a voracious reader. You always have to be ahead of your audience. I start the day by reading three newspapers, and I don't even count that as studying. That's just to keep up with current events.

How many books do you get through a year?

 Fifty to sixty in a normal year if I'm not doing research for my current book. Well over 100, if I am.

 What do you typically read?

 It depends on the book. My new book is about delusional thinking around the subjects of sex, politics, and religion in America, so for the past two years I've been studying related issues such as marriage, drugs, and the church. I've read over 200 books and conducted 114 interviews with experts on these topics. It's been a monster project, and I've enjoyed every minute of it

 Do you think it's important for speakers to read this much?

 The more you study, the more of an expert you will become. The more informed you are about the world, the more you can comment on it intelligently. Speakers are thought leaders, and I take the role very seriously. I want to be out in front and ahead of my audience on subjects related to mental toughness and critical thinking. Every serious speaker who wants to be considered a thought leader in this business should study politics, government, psychology, sociology, finance, the monetary and banking system, religion, science, and anything else that intertwines with their topic and that matters to their audience. I always want to be the most educated person in the room. That's not always the case, but that's always my goal. That's the only way I can command millions of dollars to do what I do,

Do you listen to audio programs?

Almost every day. It's another method of study for me,

Where do you do most of your thinking?

On the lake, feeding the ducks, water skiing, jet skiing or just floating around. I've launched international product campaigns from ideas I've had feeding the ducks from the boat. It's the most relaxed I've ever been in my life, and relaxation breeds creativity. In this business, you're always one idea away from another million-dollar payday. One day you dream up an idea, and the next day it's going around the world. It's a pretty amazing process.

Do you keep your goals written down. Do you have a vision statement or a vision board?

I keep a list of goals with me almost all the time to keep me on track and make adjustments. I have a ten to twenty page

detailed vision statement I update every twelve months and read every day. I currently have nine vision boards between my two homes with pictures pasted on poster boards, which I keep in my home gyms so I can see them as I work out. When I started interviewing millionaires in 1984, they told me to create vision boards. So on the weekends, I would gather magazines of fine homes, beautiful cars and luxury vacations and tape them on poster boards and hang them all over our little apartment. My friends would come over and laugh at me. That was thirty years ago. No one's laughing anymore.

As a million-dollar speaker, you're viewed as a thought leader. Do you get asked questions outside of your topic? For example, do you get asked questions on politics or current issues when you're on stage?

All the time. Once you position yourself as a thought leader and prove your skill, people want to know what you think about other areas of life. I've gone on television and radio across the country and around the world and debated doctors, lawyers, judges, politicians, and others. That's one of the reasons I study so much. Once you hit the big time of this business, your persona begins to transcend your expertise. An example is Sarah Palin. A few years ago, she was the mayor of a tiny town in nowhere Alaska, and today the press wants her opinion on everything because John McCain promoted her as a thought leader. She's been embarrassed in the press over and over because McCain promoted her as this worldly, highly educated woman, which she clearly is not. Her credibility has been destroyed over and over, yet to her credit she is attempting to bounce back by educating herself and staying in the game. The hockey moms of America seem to love her and many people in the press are giving her a third and fourth chance.

What was the biggest thing that changed for you when you became a million- dollar speaker?

Having enough money to be able to write and say whatever I believed onstage, in the press and in my books without fear. The million-dollar homes and all the other material things are fun, but my favorite part of being a millionaire is being afforded the opportunity to express my own unique point of view. I want to have my say on various topics before I die and having millions of people reading my words, watching me on TV, or seeing me onstage is the biggest kick of all. It's like the buzz from a drug that never ends and has no side effects. I think it's the coolest thing in the world.

Do you get treated differently at this level?

Oh, yes, very differently. The speaking business is made up mostly of people barely getting by. The average speaker earns $24,000 per year. So when you break into the big leagues, you are part of an extremely elite club. There are less than two hundred seven-figure non-celebrity professional speakers in the world. When you become a member of the club, every door in this business swings wide open. One day you're reading a top speakers book, and the next day you're backstage with him shooting the breeze. Million-dollar speakers are treated like rock stars.

Has being a million-dollar speaker allowed you to get away with things that the average speaker can't get away with?

Yes, but I try not to abuse it. Being a national keynoter is the most prestigious position in this business, and being a million-dollar national keynoter is the top of the line for a non-celebrity speaker. That being said, I always see myself as a vendor to the Fortune 500 sales teams I speak, train, and consult for. It's easy to get a big head in this business when you're walking around signing books, shaking hands, and being interviewed in the press every day, but the bottom line is we are only successful because of the clients we serve. I try to be friendly, humble, and easy to work with. I try to always remember where I came from and be grateful for the opportunity to serve people doing something I love. It's a true privilege to be in this business.

Some people say they love to speak and don't care about the money. They do this because it's their passion and they want to help people. Do you care about the money?

I like being a millionaire. I highly recommend it. I never have to work another day in my life. I can retire in luxury anytime I wish. It's an empowering place to be. That being said, I will likely drop dead onstage at hundred years old talking about mental toughness and critical thinking. I love it way too much to even consider doing anything else. People who say they don't care about the money are making a grave mistake, because if you're broke and always struggling for money, you can't be your best onstage and devote 100% of your attention to this business. Broke speakers waste most of their time worrying how to pay their bills instead of how to motivate and inspire their audiences. I know because I've been a broke speaker. Not only does it suck, it's stressful and totally unnecessary. The streets in this business are paved with gold, and if you're not earning at least a serious six-figure income, you're not reaching enough people with your message. Money and reach go hand-in-hand in this business. The richest speakers are reaching millions of people and changing lives. The average speaker is reaching almost no one. At the end of the day, you can only live in so many homes and drive so many cars. We all get in this business for the same reason, and that's to inspire people with our message. And until you're earning a world-class income, very few people are hearing you and the message you have such a burning desire to deliver.

 Do you think having that philosophy is part of the reason why you've become so successful?

 Yes. Speakers that deny the importance of being financially successful are kidding themselves. There's not much credibility in being broke and standing on stage telling people how to succeed, and this is a business driven by credibility. If you have the choice of being a rich speaker instead of a poor speaker, why would you choose poor? All of us have this choice.

 What's the advantage of having money in the speaking business?

 It allows you to focus on speaking and writing without wasting time worrying about how to pay the mortgage. It gives you the freedom to be a fearless thought leader while operating on the bleeding edge of the business.

Is most of your time spent in hotels and traveling from speech to speech?

No. My business model is based on leveraging every speech to its maximum potential, which means when I agree to speak for a company, I'm planning on doing years of additional training and consulting, most of which is delivered by phone. I have no interest in being a part of the speaker's circuit rat race. It's a foolish and exhausting business model.

Do you have to be available 24/7 for your clients and/or to be on the media?

I am always available to the economic buyer who hires me as a consultant, and I try to be available to go on national television 24/7, but you don't have to be. I would never expect anyone to spend the time that I do working this business. This is my life, and it's the exact life I dreamed of when I got into this business. I love it. I don't watch football on Sundays or belong to the bowling team. This business is all I think about, and it's all I want to think about.

Are you dressed up in a suit every day?

Oh, God. No! When I'm off the road, I'm on the lake almost every day, so I'm in shorts and t-shirts.

Do you have to be in the office eight hours a day or can you work wherever you like?

All I need is a computer and a cell phone and I can work anywhere.

Do you feel free at this point?

I am free to do whatever I want. This business has been very good to me. It's allowed me to live a life most people only see in movies.

Do you consider what you do "work"?

Not at all. It's more like waking up every day and remembering it's Christmas. It's so much fun, it's hard to believe we get paid for it.

It's that much fun?

It's a blast.

Do you feel fulfilled?

Yes, but the reason has little to do with money. What fulfills me is reaching millions of people around the world with my Mental Toughness message. I get a real kick out of expressing my ideas and asking people around the globe to consider them. It turns me on like nothing else I've ever experienced. Last year 100 million people heard or saw me on stage or in the media, and by the time I die, it will be in the billions. That idea excites me more than anything.

Do you think you'll ever retire?

There's an old saying in this business: "Speakers don't retire. They die." I'm going to be speaking and writing until they haul me off in a box.

Do most speakers retire?

No.

What next? Where do you want to go from here?

I'm going for mainstream celebrity. My new book is called Sex, Politics and Religion: How Delusional Thinking is Destroying America. I want to take critical thinking to the masses by applying it to the most controversial and important social issues in the country.

Is the speaking business really as good as it sounds?

It's better, but only if you're in the top tier. Most speakers are struggling and that's never fun. But at the top of the game, it's pretty spectacular.

Is there a downfall to being a top speaker?

If there is, I haven't found it.

Are there any bad parts to being in the business?

There's a dark side of the business that I don't like—the cheesy, get-rich-quick speakers telling people that success is easy. Most people who teach speaking skills have never made any serious money speaking, and most of the flashy speaker-marketing gurus only make money telling others how to make money. There are a lot of phonies out there, and that's why you have to learn from speakers who are in the business at the highest level. You have to do your homework. The industry needs to rid itself of the charlatans. They are modern-day snake oil salesman and they give the rest of us a bad name.

Is the lifestyle of a top speaker really as good as it sounds?

It is.

Any other comments on the lifestyle of being a million-dollar speaker?

If this is your dream, I think you'd be crazy not to go for it. It's a business very few people understand, including 90% of the full-time speakers. Start with a world-class education in keynote speaking, then build your skills and learn how to leverage them. Learn to how build a multidimensional business model from someone who has earned millions doing it and is still in the business. Make sure you're offering a unique point of view and valuable solution that differentiates you from the mass of speakers who are regurgitating Think and Grow Rich and How to Win Friends and Influence People. Do these things, work at it day and night, and you have a legitimate shot at the big leagues of this business. Believe me, it's worth the fight.

CONCLUSION

I hope you've enjoyed reading this book and learned as much from Steve as I did in writing it. If you didn't know who Steve Siebold was when you picked up this book, I hope you feel connected to him now and understand why I begged him to share his story and knowledge. I've learned that talent is not enough to make it in this business. If that was the case, there would be a lot more successful speakers. It's the speakers who have the knowledge and understand how the money flows that make it to the top.

I challenge you to take what you've learned from this book and apply it to your business. Have a clear vision of where you want to go and make the decision to get there. Don't let anyone get in your way. Most importantly, have fun.

I hope to share the big stage with you someday and truly wish you all the best.

Elliot Saltzman

Minneapolis, Minnesota

December 15, 2012

ABOUT THE AUTHOR

Elliot Saltzman is a speaker, author, and consultant who has shared the stage with platform legends such as Bob Proctor, Brian Tracy and Larry Wilson. At the age of 21, he earned over $50,000 in ten weeks selling door to door for a summer job. The next year, he set company records and became a six figure door to door salesperson. He later helped start a construction company and led the sales team to 2.2 million dollars in gross sales its first year. He and his wife, Jennae, live in St. Paul, Minnesota with their golden retriever Berkeley.

24022579R00138

Made in the USA
Lexington, KY
02 July 2013